Cover Page: Constable Ernest Pike
Superintendent Archibald Buchanan
Chief Constable Hoël Llewellyn
Sergeant Frank Crouch

Cover and maps by John Leftwich

MURDER FOR THE TRUTH?

by

Edwin Williamson

*"The truth is often a terrible weapon of aggression.
It is possible to lie, and even murder, for the truth."*

Alfred Adler

Murder for the Truth?

Glyn Jones (Edwin Williamson) has asserted his right under the Copyright, Designs and Patents Act 1988 to be identified as the author of this book

Orinoco Standard
Published by David Barnby, Witney
davebarnby@aol.com
Copyright © 2013

Also Published by David Barnby

Layman's Guide to the English Constitution – 2011
Land's End to John O' Groats – 2012

Introduction to the Second Edition

When I first became aware of the outline of the story of the "Netheravon Police Murder" in 1990 I was intrigued that such an event could happen in a small country parish, and I thought that the facts would be straightforward and easy to access. As I researched, it became apparent that the official versions did not stack up. The simplistic notion that a constable should, without any other pressures, commit murder and suicide because of thwarted promotion was transparently ridiculous. As I uncovered more and more facts I came to a conclusion that what I was finding should be recorded for posterity, and my notes gradually composed themselves into a narrative which I thought might be of some interest to modern readers. In 2000, unable to interest any publisher, I self-published a small run – 200 copies – of the first edition of this book, which sold gratifyingly quickly. Whilst I received plaudits from many readers, I nevertheless felt that the story had limited appeal and that the natural readership (local people, descendants, police historians and present day Wiltshire police officers) had been almost exhausted. Despite occasional requests to republish I declined to do so, on the grounds that I thought it unlikely that the rapid sales of the first edition would be repeated, and that a costly exercise in vanity would be the only result.

I should explain my connections with the Wiltshire Police: when I originally wrote this book, I had none whatsoever. Then, unexpectedly, a year or so after it was first published I took employment with them. I did not use my new employment status to advertise the book, and I kept quiet about it until my local village bobby put two and two together. He was far less reticent than me and several police employees became aware of my authorship. I have never used my position as an employee to advertise or promote this book.

In late 2012, completely out of the blue, I received a telephone call from David Barnby. David had bought a copy of the first edition more than a decade earlier, and was conscious of the approaching centenary of the policemen's deaths. He is also a published author himself, and was able to offer the chance, and facilities, to publish a second edition of 'Murder for the Truth?'. His personal drive and vision far exceed my own, and to him must go all the credit for producing this second edition.

Edwin Williamson
Haxton, Wiltshire.

March 2013

CONTENTS

Illustrations	i
Preface	iii
Map of Avon Valley	iv
Map of Coombe	v

Chapter

1.	Flash Point	1
2.	What Places! What Times!	6
3.	Trouble, Long Time Brewing	30
4.	The Cast Assembles	57
5.	Realisation. The Bodies are Discovered.	81
6.	Inquisition Super Visum Corporis	89
7.	Correspondence. Funerals, Decisions, Resolutions	106
8.	The Sort of Court. The Public Inquiry	119
9.	Drawing Breath	147
10.	Last Chance for Justice.	154
11.	Salt in the Wounds October 1913	166
12.	Awkward Questions	169
13.	Aftermath. 1913 - 2013	175
	Acknowledgements and Sources	193

ILLUSTRATIONS

Plate a: *Hoël Llewellyn as Chief Constable of Wiltshire. This photograph must have been taken after 1911, as he is wearing the ribbon of the Coronation medal, and before 1914 when he joined the army. His medals are DSO, 1911 Coronation Medal (County and Borough Police version), British South Africa Company Medal, East and West Africa medal, (see text) Queens South Africa medal and Kings South Africa medal. He is wearing the three rank stars of an army captain.*

Plate b: *Case Shot Kopje, the scene of Llewellyn's adventure with a Maxim Gun. The Matabele rushed the position from the cleft in the middle foreground. This picture was taken some hours after the fight, when the mown down bodies had been removed.*

Plate c: *Hoël Llewellyn in British South Africa Police full dress. Note that he has adopted British Royal Artillery collar badges and 'ball' pattern buttons.*

Plate d: *Ernest Pike.*

Plate e: *Superintendent Archibald Buchanan, Amesbury Police Station 1917*

Plate f: *Frank Crouch.*

Plate g: *The Phillimores outside the Three Horse Shoes, 1912. L - R, daughter Edith; who played no part in the story; Emma, Walter and Tom. This is the doorway through which Crouch claimed to have heard Pike pass at 10.30 on the night of 4th March 1913. The sun blind in the backgound protects the window of a butchers shop. Tom Phillimore stood under this before being spotted and questioned by Crouch.*

Plate h: *Frank, Alice (Kate) and Wilfred Crouch, 1904. They are standing outside their house at "Tin Town ", at Brimstone Bottom near Ludgershall. This was the accommodation village for the navvy gangs who were employed to build the army barracks at Tidworth in 1904/05. A lively spot!*

Plate i: *Chief Constable and Coroner pass the site of Pike's suicide.*

Plate j: *Hoël Llewellyn at Coombe. The original newspaper caption states that he is leaving the inquest, but in fact he appears to be coming out of the hut in Fifield where Ernest Pike's body lay.*

Plate k: *Ernest and Amelia (Millie) Pike with their four oldest children, Florence, Dorothy, Gladys and James. This picture from ca.1905 is thought to have been taken whilst the family lived in Bottlesford, where they first met the Reverend William Keating.*

Sources:

Plates a, f and h are from the Police Archives at the Wiltshire County Record Office, Trowbridge

Plate b - Robert Baden-Powell, from 'The Matebele Campaign 1896' (Methuen, London) 1897

Plate c - Somerset Leaders, by Gaskill, privately published (ND circa 1906)

Plate d - Wiltshire Telegraph

Plate e - Private collection

Plate g - Mrs Pat Oborne, executor of the estate of the late Fred Phillimore

Plates i and j - Wiltshire News

Plate k - Christopher Pike

Preface to First Edition

There has never been another case in Britain quite like that of Frank Crouch and Ernest Pike, and yet the truth behind their story remained untold. As the cover up which occurred in 1913 has been successful for a century, the two men have inevitably been remembered – if at all – only for the manner of their deaths.

The contributory factors and personalities just happened to converge in a little community in Salisbury Plain, but events could have occurred anywhere in Britain, so to understand what made men act as they did, it is necessary to look beyond the local horizon. This extends the narrative, which won't interest everybody, but each individual reader can, without disadvantage, easily skip those chapters they consider superfluous.

There is no imagined dialogue. All quotations are as reported at the time.

Haxton, Wiltshire, April 2000 Edwin Williamson

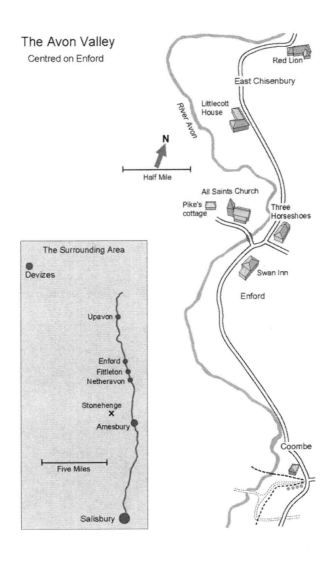

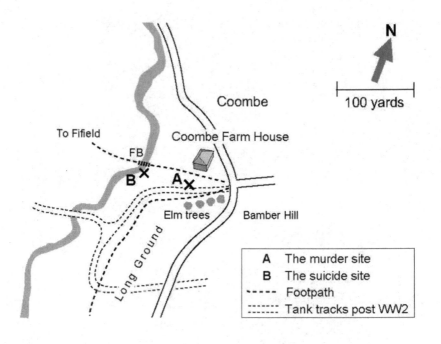

Chapter 1

Flash Point

The Avon Valley
Evening and Night of Monday 31st March 1913

Two pairs of cyclists left the new Police Divisional Headquarters at Amesbury at about 5.30 p.m. on Monday, 31st March 1913 to head north along the Avon valley. All four men were policemen, each serving a different village on the banks of the river north of the ancient abbey town which is best known for its proximity to Stonehenge. After earlier events that afternoon it was asking too much that they might all cycle companionably together as a quartet.

The first pair to leave had the farthest to ride. Constable William Slade was the representative of the law in the village of Upavon some 8 miles upstream. His companion, Constable Ernest Pike, a lean, athletic man, would accompany him most of the way, only parting company at Enford where he had been the respected and popular local bobby since February 1909. Under different circumstances it might have been a pleasant ride home, for it was the 2nd birthday of Pike's youngest child, and Ernest was a loving father. Little George Pike's five siblings aged between four and twelve would no doubt be looking forward to sharing a special birthday tea with him and their parents.

But Ernest Pike rode along in the bitter grip of gloom and shame, for a tell-tale dark patch on his sleeve bore mute witness to his humiliation. Prior to 1919 the top grade of constables wore a single 'Merit Class' chevron on the sleeve, much like that still worn by Lance Corporals in the army. Ernest had worn his stripe until that afternoon, when it had been taken from him by the Chief Constable of Wiltshire, Captain Hoël Llewellyn D.S.O.

The other pair of cyclists had not so far to go. Sergeant William Frank Crouch, a more portly man than Ernest, was returning to the village of Netheravon where since 1909 he had been the local station sergeant. His personal patch also included the village of Fittleton across the River Avon, and he had a supervisory responsibility for constables in other neighbouring villages including Ernest Pike's Enford. In the more formal manner of the times he would have been addressed by his rank and surname by most people, but was known by his middle name, Frank, to family and friends.

The charge upon which Ernest Pike had been brought before the Chief Constable had been laid by Sergeant Crouch, and the hearing had not gone smoothly.

Crouch's companion as they set off from Amesbury was P.C. Keys, and he had the shortest journey of all at about a mile for he was stationed in Durrington near Stonehenge. Keys came from the same home village as Crouch, Rowde near Devizes, where he was usually known by the different name of Jennings, an arrangement more common in those days than today for various good reasons.

As each pair separated, neither Slade nor Keys could possibly imagine the circumstances in which they would next see their particular cycling companion. Pike made some strange remarks before parting company with Slade, but the latter put this down to bluster after the unhappy events of the day, and he must have assumed that Ernest would soon settle down.

"That's it!" said Pike as he turned off the road through Enford to his cottage on the hillside near the church. *"I have done with the Force!"*

"Cool yourself man", Slade called after him. Even if much else has been forgotten, Pike's chilling rejoinder to his colleague has been remembered in the villages to this day – *"I shall make the county ring!"*

After reaching their respective homes, the men took their evening meals before setting out on their nightly patrols. Crouch had time to patrol the village street after arriving home, being seen by Harry Harding, a local groom under the Post Office clock at a little after 7.30 p.m. before returning to his flint and brick police house at the southern end of the village to prepare for his night time beat.

Bobbies of the time knew the reassurance that their presence gave to the public, so long hours were spent on the beat, and policemen were a familiar and respected sight. There were a few mounted policemen in the Wiltshire force, ex-cavalrymen who patrolled the remotest areas of the Plain on horseback, but the majority of patrols were done on foot and bicycles were kept for administrative journeys.

Beats often included a pre-arranged rendezvous with other policemen at 'conference points' on the parish boundaries which marked the limit of their areas, a system which helped liaison and the passage of information at a time when very few police stations were connected to the telephone system. Although when in his supervisory role Crouch might enter the parishes of his subordinate constables unannounced, when he was patrolling as local bobby for Netheravon and Fittleton he would meet them at the boundaries in the usual manner. In the normal course of events he was due to rendezvous with Ernest Pike at 11 p.m. that night at a spot where the boundary between the two parishes ran through the cross roads in the hamlet of Coombe. Rendezvous they would, but the course of events would be far from normal.

Crouch donned his heavy police cape, for March 1913 had been a very wet month. After a short false start he hurried back home to collect his truncheon. Mindful perhaps of Pike's display of temper at Amesbury earlier that day, he might have reflected on the constable's reputation for being a handy man with his fists.

Two miles upstream in the thatched cottage which doubled as the Pike family home and Enford Police Station, Ernest also made his arrangements for the evening patrol. Since leaving Slade, and arriving home at six o'clock he had spent the time until 9.00 writing at his desk in the front room which did service as an office. He had joined the family for tea, but any birthday joy which might have been anticipated by the children was muted by their father's downcast demeanour. Their mother Amelia (Millie) later described her husband's behaviour as 'heartbroken'.

At some point in the evening he made a sinister preparation. Whilst Amelia and the children were otherwise occupied he took his shotgun, an old fashioned double barrelled twelve bore from its usual spot in a case near the front room sofa, and unseen by anybody he placed it outside the front door of the house. At 9 p.m. he bade goodnight to his family, and leaving through the kitchen door he set off on his appointment with history. To his wife and children though, it seemed just a routine departure. They doubtless expected to hear the steady comforting tramp of his boots over the flinted roads as he returned home round about midnight. Perhaps the children hoped that daddy would not be so sad tomorrow.

Who can say what might have happened had Ernest been unsuccessful in his attempt to smuggle the gun out of the house earlier without Amelia seeing him? She would have known that he should not be carrying it whilst about his duty, and would have been alarmed given the mood of her husband that evening. He had told her of the events of the day, although shielding her from hurtful comments which had been made about her. Almost certainly she would have attempted to dissuade him from taking the gun, and perhaps even have raised an alarm amongst the neighbours which might have saved two lives. But she did not see the twelve bore. How she must have wished, over the remaining 46 years of life spent as a widow that she had been able to stop him taking it with him.

The direct route to the conference point at Coombe would have taken Crouch only 15 minutes to reach, even at a policeman's steady tramp. Ernest Pike's time would be a little longer, perhaps 25 minutes along the ancient, flint-hard road that connected the two villages in a long and gentle curve that followed a sweep in the river's course. So it is obvious that neither man was due to proceed directly there, but would have followed a prescribed route, checking houses and barns, moving on vagrants, seeing public houses closed, all the while slowly converging on Coombe for the appointed time of 11 o'clock. Beat Books from the period still exist, but they are not specific enough to tell us the exact route which both men should have followed that night.

Although there is no reliable record of either being sighted after leaving their respective homes at 9 o'clock, it is almost certain that Frank Crouch would have followed his normal beat, for he had no reason to do otherwise. What Ernest Pike did is less easy to guess at, for although he was clad in his uniform greatcoat it wouldn't have been easy to conceal the gun which any member of the public would very well know he was not permitted to carry on duty. So it seems possible that he may have tried to avoid a route where he was likely to be seen.

Whilst few locals would query their local bobby directly, for him to be seen carrying a gun might have raised an alarm that just might have frustrated his intent, and it is certain that he was leaving nothing to chance that night. Anyway, it would have required a superhuman effort of will on his part to carry out the normal checks and visits knowing, as only he did, how the night would end for him and his Sergeant. Unless of course his mind was in such a state that he could mentally accommodate the thought of carrying out his duties normally before the eleven o'clock meeting which would end two lives.

Coombe Farmhouse, which would soon play its own part in the drama, was then the home and business premises of Eustace Bertram Maton and overlooks the crossroads where the two men were to meet. At 11 o'clock that night servants at the rear of the house were not alarmed to hear two shots. It was, they thought, somebody after a rabbit or two, or possibly soldiers firing blanks. After all, the Wiltshire Territorials had been staying with the regular battalion of their regiment at nearby Tidworth recently, and men in khaki had been out on the downs all day. Little did Mr Maton's staff know, as they turned out the oil lamps and went to their beds that the corpses of two policemen now lay within yards of where they slept.

Chapter 2

What Places! What Times!
The Where ....

Of the many rivers which bear the name '*Avon*', the one which features in this story rises in the Pewsey Vale, and flows due south to meet the sea at Christchurch. Its character changes significantly at Salisbury, where there is a confluence with four streams and from there to its mouth quite large towns have grown on its banks. North of Salisbury is a different matter; all the riverside communities, with the exception of the town of Amesbury, are no more than small villages. Upstream from Amesbury, out on the Plain, they are dotted along the valley, separated from each other by a mile or so. Netheravon, Fittleton, Coombe and Enford, consecutive settlements some seven miles north of Amesbury are the sites of the story.

A centuries-old sense of isolation still existed in this part of the valley in 1913. Nature played its part, for outside of this little valley the windswept Plain stretches in all directions, but lack of modern communications contributed too; anybody looking at a map could see that the linear ribbon of communities was an ideal candidate for a railway line, and after the expansion of the permanent way in the nineteenth century, the absence of such a connection might have seemed puzzling. Plans to construct a line had in fact come very close to fruition, but had eventually been scotched by the War Office which had owned most of the land since 1897.

The military had a long association with the Plain, but only the development of weaponry, transport and communications in the final decades of the 19th century had prompted them to acquire vast tracts of freehold land. Sir Michael Hicks-Beach, Chancellor of the Exchequer, had been compelled to sell his vast Netheravon estate to the Army in 1897, and the Army Cavalry School had been established in the Park of his former great house. Huge camping grounds for visiting troops were located near Coombe, and the emergence of military aviation prompted developments near the Avon Valley.

By 1913 Enford was overlooked by the Upavon Aerodrome, and near Netheravon a new airfield was under construction for the Royal Flying Corps. On the opposite, western side of the valley lay huge artillery ranges. These establishments, whilst covering large areas of ground had comparatively small staffs, so the influx of soldiery to the valley was relatively small except during annual manoeuvres when the camping grounds filled up.

. . . . and the When

It is too easy simply to say that the incompatible personalities of the characters in this story were the sole cause of what happened, for that would be to ignore the pressures then bearing upon society and the police. Those pressures had a direct effect on what occurred, and have to he understood.

Immense power still lay with the traditional ruling classes, and they made great efforts to ensure that this should remain the case. However, since 1906 a succession of reforming Liberal administrations under Campbell-Bannerman and Asquith had been successfully battling to introduce a series of measures aimed at improving the lot of the populace at large. These struck at the almost exclusively Tory upper classes in two ways. First in their pockets, for innovations such as old age pensions and meals and health care in schools cost money, and the Liberal Chancellor, David Lloyd George was taking most of this in the form of greatly increased taxes and death duties.

Secondly, to the distaste and horror of those who felt that only their own small *élite*, the so-called 'Upper Ten Thousand', were born and bred to lead, traditional power bases were beginning to be assailed by true representatives of the masses. Even Liberal politicians were still by and large upper class patricians, not too much of a threat to the old order, but a new breed of Socialists had recently arisen and formed themselves into the Independent Labour Party. They were still ineffective at a national level, but their activities infuriated and frightened the ruling classes. Even tolerant Tories who agreed that the conditions of the poor should be relieved felt aggrieved that the Liberals had entered into secret pacts which resulted in Labour members being elected in the 1906 General Election.

Of all the blows to the old order, none was more significant than the hard won Parliament Act of 1911 which curtailed the absolute power of peers to reject legislation, and sent out an unmistakable message about the inevitable way that power was going to shift. Most of the upper class would not bow to the wind though, and resisted the changes which they saw as taking the country to the dogs. In the shire counties, site of so many aristocratic country seats, reform was very effectively blocked. Here, the attitudes and aims of the peerage were shared by the gentry, the two groups forming a power *bloc* which was determined to retain mastery in the hands of a privileged few.

They were remarkably successful, maintaining semi-medieval powers right up until the final decades of the nineteenth century. Until 1888 there was no real separation of executive and judicial powers in the counties, both functions being conjoined in the hands of the county Justices of the Peace, magistrates appointed by the Crown on the recommendation of Lords Lieutenant. A county like Wiltshire would have about two hundred and fifty Justices, and they met four times a year at Quarter Sessions not only to hear serious court cases but also to deal with purely administrative functions.[1]

Any thought of an ordinary working man being appointed to the magistrates bench was socially quite out of the question, no Lord Lieutenant was going to recommend such a thing, but just to make it certain, property and financial qualifications were imposed by law, thus ensuring that magisterial power would remain in moneyed hands.

Things started to change in the late 1880s. The increasing complication of public administration throughout the nineteenth century had spawned all sorts of independent bodies and the need for properly run, centralised authorities became obvious. In 1888 County

---

[1] Less serious court cases would be heard by local panels of magistrates sitting in Petty Sessions. Boroughs had their own magistrates.

County Councils thus came into being,[2] centralising all administrative responsibilities including those which had always previously been in the hands of the County Justices.

In theory this separated the executive and judicial functions and gave any enfranchised man the right to stand for council office, but in fact the nobility and gentry slipped easily into the most important County Council positions, and clung on tenaciously – the Marquess of Bath was Chairman of the Wiltshire County Council for 40 years, from 1906 to 1946. Owing their electoral success more to the natural deference of the voting masses than to any particular administrative talent, they used their positions to resist unwelcome government interference, especially as central grants were only a small part of their revenue.[3]

The picture may seem feudal and unappealing, but most people accepted their station in life. The English aristocracy was not brutal, simply patronising, and the lower orders of society mirrored this with their conditioned obsequiousness and deference.

The Church of England helped; clergymen came from noble or gentry stock, and were financially very comfortably placed. Firmly established as members of the ruling classes, they nevertheless had the privilege of close access to the lower orders, and enormous influence over the education of local children. Their propaganda was successful; congregations grew year on year for decades up to 1913. Only the experience of the worst war in British history would set that trend into the decline from which it has never recovered.

The couplet, "*God bless the Squire and his relations, and keep us in our proper stations*", put the system in a nutshell, at least in rural areas, and children in Sunday schools would trill the lines later omitted from most hymn books,

> "*The rich man in his castle,
> the poor man at his gate,*

---

[2] Local Government Act 1888.
[3] In 1913 Central Government Grants represented only 14% of Local Government revenue.

> *God made them high or lowly,*
> *He ordered their estate."*

Such a society encouraged an unquestioning deference to those in positions of power. They, in their turn, were absolutely certain of their innate superiority, and the sense of their own decency convinced them that they behaved out of a sense of duty, not personal gratification. They knew what was best for the lesser classes, and they felt a responsibility to impose it, having as they saw it, the birth, breeding and training which enabled them to make the right decisions. Not infrequently they felt justified in breaking or ignoring the laws of the land, the main purpose of which were to keep the masses in order, if their superior sensitivities told them that it was best to do so in the interests of the country or of society. Even the Prince of Wales could go into a witness box and perjure himself, and remain assured that his crime would be seen as an act to protect the monarchy. The fact that it also got him off an embarrassing hook didn't come into it, of course.

Primus et Optimus

The history of organised British mainland police forces commences with the founding of the Metropolitan Police by Sir Robert Peel in 1829, and during the following decade a number of city and borough constabularies were formed. Outside the urban centres though, there was still nothing like a police force, and rural crime detection was largely a personal responsibility. Maintenance of public order was fulfilled by recourse to the army, usually the irregular militia and yeomanry whose crowd control techniques usually resulted in bloodshed.

Southern rural counties including Wiltshire had suffered from widespread discontent in the early 1830s, the 'Captain Swing' riots, which were eventually suppressed by the use of yeomanry and harsh punishments. No sooner had this problem been resolved than the Chartist movement raised the spectre of large scale civil disobedience in town and country. Their aims were socially just, viewed from a modem standpoint, but their methods were flawed by a readiness to resort to violence; "*peacefully if we can*", they declared, "*but by force if we must*".

In May 1839 leaflets began to appear in Wiltshire urging public violence in the towns of Devizes, Trowbridge and Melksham. The Yeomanry were mobilised, and the County Magistrates wisely requested the assistance of a detachment from the Metropolitan Police. The courageous self-restraint of these 20 unarmed men from 'A' Division of the capital's constabulary made its mark on the Wiltshire authorities, and when the County Police and District Constabulary Act passed by Parliament in 1839 gave shires the right to form constabularies if they wished, the Wiltshire Justices were quick off the mark. Meeting at Quarter Sessions in October, they approved the raising of a force. The wisdom of their decision was soon confirmed by events in Monmouthshire in early November when the militia killed twenty armed Chartists who had attempted to seize the town of Newport. Back in Wiltshire, the County Constabulary came into being on 28th November, the first such force in Britain, a fact commemorated today by their motto '*Primus et Optimus*', (First and Best).[4] It was a close run thing though, as three other counties had forces in being within two weeks. The 1839 Act was entirely permissive, and there was no compulsion upon local authorities to form forces until 1856.[5]

The new forces were by no means universally welcomed, even by the law abiding majority, being seen in many quarters as an unwelcome expense, a tool of the ruling classes or as a 'French-style' threat to civil liberties. In many districts the first constables were even reluctant to wear uniforms for fear of being assaulted, and in a truly disgraceful case in London in 1833 the sour public feeling was shown by an inquest verdict of justifiable homicide on a constable who was stabbed whilst policing a political meeting.[6] In 1841, only eighteen months after the

---

[4] The small Salisbury City Constabulary had been in existence for some years previously under Borough Police legislation.

[5] County and Borough Police Act 1856.

[6] P.C. Robert Culley, killed at Coldbath Fields Clerkenwell. Fortunately this perverse result, reached against the coroner's direction and the weight of evidence, was quashed by the King's Bench.

formation of the Wiltshire force a petition asking for its abolition received huge support from every single parish in the county.

Control of the police in borough forces fell to the lot of Watch Committees, ancient bodies which for centuries had held responsibility for peace in towns and became the obvious supervisory authorities once constabularies came into being. No comparable body existed at county level though, and the County Justices took control of the forces as they did with all administrative affairs. The Act granted them the right to appoint Chief Constables who were to be given wide ranging disciplinary powers over subordinates, and the County Justices set about looking for suitable candidates with experience of controlling large bodies of disciplined men. The Metropolitan Police could not be called upon to provide a pool of suitable officers, and so the solution was to invite military or naval officers to apply. Wiltshire appointed Captain Samuel Meredith R.N., beginning a sequence of over 105 years in which all its Chiefs would be ex-naval officers.

As the century progressed there was concern about whether the police should be an arm of the judiciary or the executive, but as both functions were combined at county level within the persons of the Justices the debate was sterile. However, the introduction of elected County Councils provided a meaningful stimulus to the argument, and police provisions within the 1888 Act brought about the hybrid bodies which were to control county forces for the next eight decades – the Standing Joint Committees.

Examples of the British *penchant* for compromise, these committees shared police control between appointed magistrates and elected county council members, but they had not come into being without resistance from the House of Lords. Nearly all of Their Lordships were Justices in their county retreats, and their entirely predictable opinion that control of the police should remain with the magistracy was supported by many on the Conservative side of the lower House, where the sons of the aristocracy filled the benches. When it became clear though, that the will of the majority of the elected chamber was that control was to be shared, a rear-guard fought to reserve at least the specific power of appointing chief constables solely to the J.P.s on the new committees. This divisive motion which would have relegated elected committee men to a second-class position was defeated, but the victory was hollow, for when the S.J.C.s came into being, the magisterial social *élite* took control of the new committees, dominating them by force of personality, money, and status. The balance between elected councillors and appointed magistrates was not as was intended either, for many J.P.s also held elected council seats, and qualified for S.J.C. places on that secondary basis with the result that the proportion of magistrates was in excess of the 50 per cent which Parliament intended.

After the end of the First World War S.J.C.s were increasingly standardised and regulated and they survived until 1964 when new police authorities replaced them. In 1913, though bound by Home Office guidelines in some areas, they still had a great deal of jealously guarded independence over the way that they recruited, administered, disciplined and paid their respective forces. The disproportionate social composition of S.J.C.s inevitably meant that they became concentrated hives of the resentment towards Liberal changes. They were going to run things their way for as long as they could, and they were going to select Chief Constables from their own class who saw eye to eye with them.

This caused a steady and bitter flow of complaints from ordinary coppers about the antiquated disciplinary code based on the 1839 Act, which ruled so much of their working and private lives, and about the preference of S.J.C.s for ex-military Chief Constables. As the years had gone by this requirement had become increasingly detrimental to morale, as the best professional policemen had become well suited through length of service and experience, but Standing Joint Committees 'knew a gentleman when they saw one' and clung to their outdated selection requirement. Many Army and Navy officers, with breath-taking confidence in their own gifted amateurism, contrived to attach themselves in unspecified ways to police forces for a few months in order to learn the ropes before applying for Chief Constableships, and some, in tacit admission of their own uselessness at the outset of their new career, would offer to forgo salary for some months until they were, by their own assessment, ready for the job.

By the turn of the century this lunacy was starting to change, but in 1908, the year of Llewellyn's appointment, only 12 per cent of county Chief Constables had risen from the ranks. The top policemen served for amazing lengths of time too – the first Chief Constable of Surrey was aged eighty-six at the time of his retirement in 1899 – so that the effect of the old selection methods were felt for many years after more meritocratic criteria had been introduced and men appointed in the old way continued in office in county constabularies until the 1940s. The Metropolitan Force perpetuated the old system longest; it was not until 1958, with the appointment of Sir Joseph Simpson, that a professional policeman became Commissioner.[7]

County Chief Constables were allowed to impose a range of disciplinary sanctions on their subordinates, from small fines to instant dismissal with loss of pension rights, and within these parameters their powers were unfettered. In a crucial difference between the two types of force, a borough constable might appeal to the Watch Committee, but a county bobby was denied any such right. A Standing Joint Committee could not interfere in the disciplinary decisions reached by their Chief Constables, even if they felt inclined to do so. They could, *in extremis*, dismiss a Chief but this was hardly a tool of control for matters that did not call for such a drastic sanction, and anyway, it was unthinkable that a working class policeman's complaint might bring about the downfall of a gentleman Chief Constable. The 'one man system' as it came to be known was usually administered in an unfair and arbitrary way as a means of imposing control and reinforcing the position of the hierarchy rather than as a fair means of maintaining discipline, any disagreement over facts invariably being decided in favour of the senior rank.

---

[7] The Metropolitan Police Commissioner was the equivalent of a Chief Constable. Confusingly the Met also had a rank of 'Chief Constable' for some years, but this officer was subordinate to the Commissioner.

An isolated official expression of concern about the system occurred in Devon 1881, when the Justices at Quarter Sessions expressed their disquiet that "*the Chief Constable seems to have uncontrolled command of the police force*", but in general the County Magistrates, S.J.C. and their Chief Constables saw it to be in their mutual best interests to defend the system against any change. Given the backgrounds of their chiefs, the lower ranks were inclined to claim that discipline so patently inappropriate for the police, was 'military-style', but in point of fact this was to be unfair to the army; at least a soldier could refuse to accept summary jurisdiction and ask to be tried by court-martial, where he might be legally represented, and if found guilty have the finding and sentence reviewed. With no means of redress, and victimisation commonplace, constables found it best to keep their complaints quiet, else it would be entered as a mark against them. It was felt in some quarters that recruiting Chief Constables from outside the force would help prevent internal corruption but this argument ignored the upper class cronyism between Chiefs and county authorities.

Forbidden the right to organise to represent themselves, it was inevitable that clandestine groups would start to form within the police, and the case of an officer in the Met, Inspector John Syme, provided a catalyst in 1909. Syme was an absolutely honest, dour, Presbyterian Scot who came into conflict with his superiors over his handling of a minor case. Enraged to the point of imbalance by their grossly unfair treatment, he threatened a senior officer, and was consequently dismissed and sent to prison for six months.

On release he helped to form an unofficial union known at first as 'The John Syme League', which by 1913 had become the National Union of Police and Prison Officers, membership of which would result in instant dismissal for serving officers. In due course the executive committee expelled Syme, for they perceived that he was obsessed by his own case. He unwisely libelled the Met Commissioner, Sir Edward Henry, who was in fact a sympathetic and kind man, though badly advised.[8]

---

[8] Sir Edward was sympathetic to the plight of ordinary policemen, and a man of exceptional moral principle. 'Sam Buck' (a pseudonym), in a letter printed in the *Police Review* of 18th

Nevertheless, Syme was not without powerful friends, who expended much effort on keeping this honest but now volatile man from the consequences of his own temper, and in 1924 they succeeded in forcing a judicial inquiry into his complaints. He was completely vindicated, and was eventually (1931) awarded his pension backdated to the date of his dismissal in 1909. However, by a cynical distortion, the judges, whilst accepting that he had been correct in every respect in his handling of the 1909 case which had set the whole sorry business in motion, would not admit the obvious fact that his superiors had been at fault in dismissing him. No disciplined force, they said, could allow its men to exercise their right to appeal to Parliament![9] Syme became unbalanced, and took to expressing himself by throwing bricks though the windows of government offices, including 10 Downing Street. When he died in 1945, his friends in the House of Commons called him the most honest man they ever knew. It is telling that a man referred to in Parliament as 'The Soul of Honour' could be at such odds with the system of police discipline in pre-Great War England.

A Ray of Hope, John Kempster and his Magazine

In January 1893 John Kempster founded the *Police Review and Parade Gossip*, published from offices in Red Lion Square in London. There had been similar publications before this, principally the *Police Service Advertiser* founded in 1866 which became the *Police Guardian* in 1872, but the *Police Review* was destined to become the best known and most effective organ for promoting the cause of the ordinary bobby. Kempster had become acquainted with a number of policemen, and was disturbed by their treatment, telling a House of Commons Select Committee in 1908 that no individual constable dared make a complaint against his superiors.

July 1913, quotes Henry's instructions to senior officers to "*Be kind to the men*". For many years unknown to the public, Henry quietly supported the aged mother of a distraught man who had made an attempt to kill him. He was immensely saddened by the strikes which occurred in his force shortly before his retirement, and resigned in their wake.

[9] One of the judges was Rayner Goddard, later to become Lord Chief Justice, and a man known for manipulating proceedings to achieve the desired result, as his now discredited conduct in the infamous 1952 trial of Derek Bentley and Christopher Craig was to show. Goddard will appear fleetingly again in these pages.

The *Police Review* was to be their mouthpiece, and it was also a practical magazine in many ways, providing help and exercises for self-improvement and promotion examinations. As an offshoot of the magazine Kempster also set up the Police and Citizens Friendly Association in 1894, to 'promote increased confidence between police and public, and to advance the well-being and efficiency of the Police Service in the United Kingdom', for he did not support the idea of a police union which the John Syme Leaguers called for. He favoured a Police Federation with lesser powers than those traditionally claimed by a trade union, but this particular idea failed to find a response. When he sent out 21,000 application forms in 1913, only 100 were returned. History has, however, vindicated Kempster's approach.

The magazine provided an outlet for policemen's grievances. Letters were always published under pseudonyms for protection against official reprisal, and even making allowances for malcontents who may be found in any large organisation, copies of the period make sorry reading, revealing a deeply unsettled service manned by dedicated yet mistreated men. Chief Constables usually chose to ignore the Review. Men of their class felt it beneath them to respond to criticism levelled at them by their inferiors, so a short but acrimonious correspondence between Llewellyn and Kempster published in the aftermath of the Coombe deaths was extremely rare, and indicates how necessary Llewellyn thought it to be to stifle open comment *of this particular incident* in this 'subversive' periodical.

By 1913 the long campaign spearheaded by the *Police Review* and a few sympathetic Members of Parliament had achieved some heartening progress; in 1912, of 22 Chief Constables appointed throughout the country, 19 had been internally promoted and much more significantly (for it will form a backdrop to the Coombe deaths) a Police Act Amendment Bill was before Parliament, the very first section of which addressed the 'one man system'. It recommended that a county Chief Constable's power to remove a subordinate be limited to suspension, the power to dismiss being reserved to S.J.C.s.[10] The man who

---
[10] The Bill was not enacted.

exercised those widely criticised powers in Wiltshire is a key figure in the drama, and an impressive, but flawed man. It is time to have a much closer look at him.

Captain Hoël Llewellyn D.S.O.

In January 1908 Captain Robert Sterne RN stepped down from his position as Chief Constable and seven ex-military and naval men applied to fill it. At one point it looked very much as though Lord Heytesbury, then a major in the Wiltshire Regiment would gain the position, after all, he was a Wiltshire aristocrat whose uncle, Lieutenant Colonel the Honourable E.A. Holmes à Court had been Oxfordshire's first Chief Constable. Surprising many though, including Kempster of the *Police Review*, Heytesbury was beaten to it by Captain Hoël Llewellyn D.S.O.

Born at Langford Court, a country house near Burrington in Somerset on 24th November 1871, Hoël Llewellyn was the third of five sons of Evan Henry Llewellyn, a land-owner whose family wealth derived from coal and tin mining in South Wales. Evan was sufficiently wealthy to be able to purchase Langford Court at the age of 22, and he subsequently went on to become the Tory M.P. for North Somerset.

Most of his sons were sent to Radley, the public school at Abingdon in Oxfordshire, but Hoël was privately tutored until he joined the Royal Navy as a cadet at the age of twelve. Gazetted midshipman a couple of months before his sixteenth birthday he went to sea for four years and saw active service against Arab slave traders near Zanzibar whilst serving aboard the 4000 ton light cruiser HMS *Boadicea*, Captain Curzon-Howe, flag ship of the East Indies Station. 327 members of *Boadicea's* company were awarded the coveted East and West Africa Medal, with clasp '*Witu 1890*' after their involvement in a punitive expedition in October 1890.

Llewellyn, who had been noted for earlier brave conduct in the taking of a slave dhow near Pemba on 6th November 1888, was not entitled to this medal though, for in September 1889 he had been drafted to the Mediterranean, joining HMS *Undaunted*, Captain Lord Charles

Beresford, in February 1890. Nevertheless, as may be seen in later official police portraits, he took to wearing the medal ribbon which was, in fact, a summary offence under the 1888 Army Act. In December 1892 he was required to leave the Royal Navy after thrice failing to pass his Lieutenancy examinations,[11] but whilst serving he had acquired an expertise with the Maxim machine gun, a skill which would influence his life and cause him to become a policeman.

After his humiliating ejection from the Navy, he followed his eldest brother's footsteps to Rhodesia to take a post as a Government surveyor, a surprising career option for a young man who could not pass his naval mathematics examinations.[12]

Plate a. Captain Hoël Llewellyn, Chief Constable of Wiltshire

Concurrent with his arrival the Matabele War started, a conflict waged by Cecil Rhodes' British South Africa Company as a means of acquiring land from indigenous inhabitants. The Matabele were a warrior tribe of Zulu stock, and the colonists, vastly outnumbered and without aid from regular troops, knew what they were up against. They could not hope to match Africans on foot and so their forces were entirely horsed, but their great hope lay in the recently introduced Maxim machine gun which was as yet untested in combat. There had

---

[11] National Archives ADM/196/43 page 244. He should only have been allowed one attempt.
[12] The Surveyor General of Rhodesia, and Chief Magistrate in Bulawayo was Andrew F. Duncan, an ex-RN officer who, like Llewellyn, had served aboard *Boadicea*.

been earlier machine guns, notably Gatlings, Gardners and Nordenfelts, but these had all been mechanically operated, hand cranked weapons. The Maxim was the first true recoil operated automatic weapon taken into service. Firing a .45" calibre bullet at the rate of 600 rounds per minute it lived up to all expectations, enabling the colonists to inflict wholesale slaughter at little cost to themselves.

The newly arrived Llewellyn's expertise with the weapon was as fortuitous for him as it was to be lethal to the Matabele, and he was granted a commission in the Salisbury Horse, an irregular unit of Company employees, being given command of the machine guns. It is no exaggeration to say that the weapon won Rhodesia for the Empire, and Llewellyn was its principal exponent there. *'Whatever happens we have got the Maxim Gun, and they have not'*, wrote Hilaire Belloc, in cynical criticism of the use of the latest military hardware against technologically unsophisticated enemies.[13]

In early 1894 the officer in charge of all artillery and machine guns, a seconded Royal Artillery captain named Lendy, died when he burst a blood vessel whilst shot putting on the sports field, and so Llewellyn gained an unexpected promotion, and was consequently tasked with writing a report on the gun's performance to the manufacturers. He made it clear that the colonists' principal fear had lain in being overrun by huge enemy rushes, but that the Maxim had quite solved that particular problem.[14] At the end of the fighting he returned to his surveying duties, but as the Company was forced to expand its permanent police forces and maintain volunteer military units, it would seem that Llewellyn retained a degree of military status.

In early 1896 Rhodesia was almost entirely denuded of police when the Company Administrator, Dr Jameson led most of them on an ill-starred raid into the Boer Republic of Transvaal, a country then at peace with the British Empire. They were ignominiously defeated and captured, their release being conditional upon their enforced

---
[13] Hilaire Belloc, 'The Modern Traveller' 1898.
[14] Llewellyn Papers, National Army Museum 9702-13, folios 2 and 3.

return to their countries of origin, in most cases Great Britain.[15] The Matabele tribe took advantage of this weakness to rebel against white

Plate b. Case shot Kopje. *Robert Baden Powell, from 'The Matabele Campaign 1896' (Methuen, London 1897).* The Matabele were concealed in the cleft in the middle distance. Their bodies had been removed before this photograph was taken.

rule. Their cause had justice, but their tactics were brutal, and gave the white colonists a pretext for a bloody response of which the Maxim guns were again to be a principal instrument.[16] Volunteer forces were rapidly raised, the expelled policemen trickled back, and a small number of regular British troops were sent to help them put down the rebels in a campaign which saw a great deal of viciousness on both sides. Both sides routinely executed prisoners, including women and children, villages were destroyed as a matter of routine and when the rebellion spread to Mashonaland the Shona men, women and children, were dynamited when they took refuge in caves.

[15] It is possible that Llewellyn missed becoming involved in the Jameson Raid for health reasons. In July 1895 he had been sent to England to recuperate from malaria.
[16] Some idea of the importance of the weapon can be gained from the name of one of the earliest hotels in Bulawayo – 'Maxim's'.

On 5th August 1896 Llewellyn was involved in an operation at Sikombo's stronghold, which was to be remembered as the principal engagement of the campaign. Some light artillery and the Maxims had been detached from the main force to a hilltop gun position from which they could bombard the enemy. Unbeknown to them, a nearby fold in the ground had hidden a large group of tribesmen who were thus able to rush the guns. Under this sudden and unexpected threat Llewellyn gave ill-considered orders which resulted in the gunners abandoning their position to the enemy, and the rebels looked certain to capture a Maxim. Realising the danger 24 year old Hoël raced back to the position and managed to bring the gun into action when the tribesmen were only 15 yards away, He broke up the attack single-handedly, mowing down scores at point blank range and firing 900 rounds of the bone-smashing .45″ calibre ammunition in the process.[17]

Llewellens's courage in a perilous situation cannot be denied though. The Matabele were armed with relatively modern Martini-Henry rifles which they used to good effect – at one point Llewellyn was blinded by splinters thrown off by bullets striking rocks close to his head, and an 18 year old trooper named Evelyn Holmes was severely wounded as he tried to reach his officer. Holmes, the son of a colonel in the Welch Regiment, underwent the amputation of a bullet smashed leg and died a few days later.

In due course the general commanding all forces in Rhodesia commended Llewellyn for conspicuous gallantry, a term understood to be tantamount to a recommendation for the award of the Victoria Cross. No such award was made, which is almost certainly due to the fact that, brave though his act had undoubtedly been, he was simply doing his duty in retrieving a desperate situation which had been brought about by his own orders. Llewellyn should have thanked his stars that he had not been responsible for a humiliating disaster, but

---

[17] Llewellyn's attitude and enthusiasm for the work is unpleasantly hinted at in a letter of congratulations (datelined Bulawayo, 7th August 1896) which he received from Lord Grey, the Administrator for Rhodesia, in which Grey wrote: "*Once again you have shown that you are never happier than when you see the whites of the niggers' eyes*". Llewellyn Papers, folio 6).

for the rest of his life he told a flattering version of events, emphasising his own courage but never alluding to the real reason why his act of desperate bravery had been necessary.[18]

Another reorganisation of the Company forces in late 1896 resulted in the formation of the British South Africa Police, and Llewellyn was a founder member of this outstanding force which remained in existence until the creation of the modern state of Zimbabwe in 1980. When the Boer War broke out at the end of 1899, Hoël, now a 28 year old captain was in charge of the artillery of the Rhodesian forces. On 25th November 1899 he took part in a discreditable incident near the Bechuanaland/Transvaal border, when an African chief name Linchwe was persuaded, by promise of arms and ammunition to join a Rhodesian force in an attack on the Boer town of Derdepoort. In the event the Rhodesians failed to support Linchwe's warriors, and stood by and watched whilst they ran riot through the town. The action caused outrage all round. The Boers were incensed by the thought of black

Plate c: Captain Hoël Llewellyn. British South Africa Police. Officer Commanding Rhodesian Artillery and Machine Guns.

---

[18] Decisions concerning the award of the medal to BSA Company employees had, since July 1896, to be referred to the Colonial Secretary (PRO WO/32/8155) and were not within the control of the War Office. I am indebted to Mr Ian Cross, formerly a senior Resident Magistrate in Rhodesia, and currently of Pietermaritzburg, South Africa for his analysis of contemporary reports of the Sikombo's incident which reveals Llewellyn's full role. An intriguing note appended to a newspaper report of the official despatch in the Llewellyn papers at the National Army Museum (9702-13 folio 15) states; '*the truth is that the (Maxim) crew deserted and fled when they were surprised by Matabeles*'. Unfortunately this highly illuminating annotation is unattributed. It is definitely not in Llewellyn's handwriting.

men being incited against them, the British considered the action to have been precipitate, and Chief Linchwe was aggrieved at the way his warriors had been abandoned by the whites. The principal blame for the incident should go to the Rhodesian column's commanding officer, Colonel Holdworth, but Llewellyn who took a part in the decisions, was subsequently unrepentant and defensive.[19]

After commanding armoured trains on the Bulawayo line north of Mafeking, he took part in the famous relief of that besieged town, shortly after which the Rhodesian forces were withdrawn from operations against the Boers as there were again signs of native unrest, but Llewellyn was not out of the fighting for long. He was awarded the Distinguished Service Order on 29th November 1900 and in early 1901 he transferred to the newly raised South African Constabulary which was immediately thrown into the guerrilla fighting that unexpectedly followed the end of the conventional phase of the war.

Hoël saw out hostilities in charge of a column of mounted infantry and commanded the Lichtenburg District of occupied Transvaal, where he was appointed Justice of the Peace in 1902. Peace came at the end of May 1902, and in September he took some well-earned home leave. In October he married for the first time. Rather unusually for those days, his bride, Winifred, was a divorcée,[20] her marriage to Sir Charles Henry Ross (famous as a designer of Canadian rifles which bore his name) having been dissolved in 1897.

It was clearly a time to consider the future, and Llewellyn made his decision not to return to Africa, submitting his resignation from the South African Constabulary in December 1902. In four campaigns in southern and eastern Africa Llewellyn had gained a deserved reputation as a brave and loyal man to which he would honourably add in two world wars. But this appraisal must now be balanced by recognition of the character flaws which he displayed on a number

---

[19] Llewellyn's excuses were singled out for criticism in the Boer account '*Die Beleg van Mafeking*', reprinted in '*Rhodesia Served The Queen*' (Vol 1) by Colonel AS Hickman (Government Printer Salisbury, Rhodesia, 1970). See also letter written by Llewellyn in 'Rhodesia' magazine, 1st June 1901.

[20] The divorce rate in Great Britain at the time was one in every four hundred marriages.

of occasions, especially as they indicate a predisposition to the sort of behaviour of which he will stand accused in subsequent pages of this book. Possibly as a result of his early rejection by the Navy he would not brook criticism, and defended himself vigorously against any suggestion of it. There are also very strong suspicions that he was vain and arrogant, willing to embellish the truth where it suited his purpose.[21] This may not be an uncommon shortcoming among ambitious young men but it can be particularly dangerous in one who wields the sort of uncheckable powers that county Chief Constables then enjoyed. But for now this lies in the future; having established a name for himself in Africa, Hoël now had to start again in England.

Despite having nominally been a police officer for some years, his actual experience had been of irregular military operations, as far away from the work of an English constabulary as could be, but he was a determined man who had an enormous number of personal contacts, either of his own making, or through his father who was still, at this time, a Member of Parliament. He was always a string puller, and this no doubt helped him to arrange unofficial attachments to police forces in pursuance of his ambition to take a Chief Constable's appointment.

Settling first at Stanborough Bury near Hatfield, he spent almost a year with the Hertfordshire Constabulary, and then from October 1904 to April 1905 with the City of London force, before associating himself in some unspecified way with the Metropolitan Police for two months, where he familiarised himself with the system of fingerprint classification introduced by Edward Henry, the Met Commissioner since March 1903. Henry, who had been a member of the Indian Civil Service (where he trialled his fingerprint system with the Calcutta Police), had been appointed Assistant Commissioner in May 1901, moving up to the top job less than two years later. Between 1899 and 1901 however he had been seconded from India to a position in Transvaal, where he worked in Johannesburg and Pretoria reorganising the Police and overseeing the introduction of fingerprints on passes

---

[21] A further example is alluded to in '*Rhodesia served The Queen*', in which it is suggested that Llewellyn grossly exaggerated his own part in the report of an incident on 21st October 1899 when he fired on a Boer raiding party from his armoured train.

for black labourers. It is very probable that Llewellyn and Henry may have met there at this time, though there is no direct evidence of this.

It seems that at least two early job applications, for the Chief Constableships of Somerset and Worcestershire were completely unsuccessful, but by 1906 Llewellyn was starting to be short listed for appointments. Having managed to find time for a course with the London Fire Brigade, he made application to be its Chief Officer in succession to Captain Hamilton, Royal Navy (retired)[22]. He went on to apply for the Chief Constable posts of Shropshire and Devonshire before being the successful candidate selected by the Wiltshire Standing Joint Committee on 9th April 1908.[23] His personal testimonials from this period make impressive reading more for the identity of the authors than for what they wrote:

- Herbert Plumer, who had been his direct superior in Matabeleland and before Mafeking described him as "outstanding", praise indeed coming from the highly regarded soldier who was to become by common consent Britain's best commander in the Great War, a Field Marshal and Viscount. Plumer stated that as a major he had initiated the Victoria Cross recommendation in 1896.

- The Duke of Abercorn, a director of the British South Africa Company who succeeded Cecil Rhodes as Chairman, wrote a more formal testimonial, but it was potentially of great use because of useful family connections. Abercorn's sister, Lady Maud Hamilton, had married the 5th Marquess of Landsdowne, who amongst many other things was Lord Lieutenant of Wiltshire.[24]

---

[22] The Chief of the London Fire Brigade was usually appointed from ex Royal Navy Officers.
[23] In a swipe against the culture of secrecy which permeated much official county business, the *Devizes Gazette* of 16th April 1908 complained about the selection procedure carried out by the S.J.C. being far less open than that used at Quarter Sessions thirty-seven years earlier, when Sterne had been appointed. Llewellyn's insistence on referring to his fruitless V.C. recommendation caused potential embarrassment when the paper mistakenly reported in the same issue that he was a holder of the medal.
[24] Helpful connections went further: Llewellyn's father was a great personal friend and parliamentary colleague of the 5th Marquis of Bath, Chairman of the Wiltshire County Council (see letter from Lord Bath, '*Wiltshire Gazette*' 12th April 1945).

- Robert Baden-Powell, national hero and founder of the Boy Scout movement added to the praise. 'B-P' knew Llewellyn well, and had generously mentioned his Sikombo exploit in a best-selling account of the Matabele campaign.[25] Llewellyn was a member of the force which relieved Mafeking where Baden-Powell had been besieged, and he immediately transferred to the South African Constabulary on its formation by Baden-Powell in 1901.
- Sir Leander Starr Jameson, Prime Minister of Cape Colony was an impressive referee.[26]
- Admiral Lord Charles Beresford, a Lord of the Admiralty and a Conservative Member of Parliament, under whom Llewellyn had served as a midshipman aboard H.M.S. *Undaunted* in the Mediterranean completed the folio of personal recommendations.[27]

Llewellyn started to make his mark immediately, his style of command fitting the mould about which the *Police Review* and its contributors so often despaired. A stream of orders, many of which were concerned with the niceties of discipline rather than policing efficiency was soon forthcoming from his office in Devizes. He circulated strict instructions about the standard of saluting, how to wear the police issue whistle, and in one of his first general orders in May 1908 he ordered all ranks to watch out for him touring the county in his blue 10 HP Benz motor car, registration number AM1, 'with Cape Cart hood.'[28] Constables

---

[25] 'The Matabele Campaign 1896' by R.S.S. Baden-Powell (Methuen, 1897).

[26] In accordance with the terms of his release from captivity in Transvaal, Jameson had been tried in London under the Foreign Enlistment Act 1870 and sentenced to 15 months penal servitude. Released after 6 months on 'health grounds', he returned to a political career in South Africa, became Progressive Party leader and Prime Minister in 1904. He died in 1917, tight lipped to the end about official knowledge of his abortive 1895 Raid. He was considered an imperial hero by many, a buccaneering rogue by others.

[27] The Beresford family was also related to Landsdowne through marriage. In addition to his prominence as an Admiral and sitting M.P., Lord Charles was also in the public eye as the leader of a significant faction in the Royal Navy, united in their opposition to the great naval reformer Admiral 'Jackie' Fisher.

[28] The Llewellyn family seem to have been fond of motor cars. Hoël's brother Owen was a well-known motoring journalist who wrote for 'The Autocar' under the pen name 'Owen John'. Owen's great grandson is the Conservative politician, David Cameron.

were to report sightings in their pocket books, no doubt after saluting in the prescribed manner. Some of Llewellyn's instructions positively detracted from the efficiency of the force, the most ridiculous being a ban on constables conversing with civilians, which was instituted in November 1908. For years most constables, realising the benefits that sound intelligence brought, had been working hard to build up good relationships with the populace, but now a policeman on his beat who might chance to encounter any civilian, was not permitted to converse unless it was in the strict line of duty.

"*On several occasions I have dropped across members of the Force talking with civilians.*" wrote Llewellyn "*This must cease at once and I shall deal severely with any member of the Force who I find not complying with this order*".

Disciplinary action for breaches of this ruling commenced almost immediately, the first case being brought before Llewellyn in January 1909. 10 years later, even after divisive attitudes had been softened by the experience of war, a constable at Ludgershall, a village on the south eastern boundary of the county, was punished for mixing with civilians: his sin had been to play cricket with a local team during off duty hours!

Already a policeman had to seek permission before getting married, providing character references for his bride to be, but Llewellyn tightened these rules. In February 1911 he issued an order which said:

"*Members of the Force are not, when in uniform, to take their wives out for a walk or to walk with any female unless in duty bound to do so. Should a member of the force find an opportunity to take his wife for a walk he should do so in plain clothes*".

Paul Sample, in his generally uncritical 150th Anniversary anecdotal history of the Wilts Force, '*Oldest and Best*', includes this unattributed, and generously phrased quotation about the period:

'*Discipline was imposed rigorously, and perhaps not always to the benefit of the Force*'.

Nor was Llewellyn's style simply inflicted on his police subordinates and their wives; his neighbours got a taste too. He made his first home in the county at the Manor House at Conock, a small settlement a few miles south east of Devizes, where he decided to block a footpath over his land. That this was resented locally is evidenced by the fact that he found it necessary to post a guard of two constables to watch the barbed wire fences which he had erected, to ensure they were not pulled down, and this eventually resulted in a fracas in November 1909 when two village men ended up being charged with assaulting the policemen.

Llewellyn's attitude towards discipline can be excused to a large extent, for he was a man of his times carrying out his duties as expected and approved of by the Standing Joint Committee to which he owed responsibility. Conditions were similar in nearly all other county forces and in fairness it has to be said that if Llewellyn was disciplinarily inflexible, then he was an imaginative innovator in many other ways.

But the light of progressive man-management had been revealed to him, had he wished to respond to it. As an officer in the South African Constabulary he had encountered the very enlightened system of discipline introduced by the force's founder, his friend Robert Baden-Powell who typically placed great emphasis on fair treatment, self-reliance and open access between all ranks, as long as they were white. Of course Llewellyn could not fully and immediately introduce such radical changes to the Wiltshire force, but there is no sign that he even wished to temper the strict regime of which so many rightly complained. In fact, he tightened the screw, and firmly defended his unaccountability, being fully supported in this by the S.J.C.

It was an opportunity missed; technically innovative though he may have been, Llewellyn failed to see the relationship between Chief Constables and their men was ripe for change. There would be enormous prices to pay for such intransigence in all forces around the country, but no price would be sadder than the unnecessary deaths of two good men in Wiltshire.

Chapter 3

Trouble, Long Time Brewing

After a gap of one hundred years it is well-nigh impossible to try and peer into the mind of a man like Ernest Pike, yet his homicidal frenzy on the night of 31st March 1913, seemingly so disproportionate to the events which provoked them, cry out for some attempt at explanation of his character.

Police Constable Number 7 Ernest Pike. Born at Lower High Street, Malmesbury on 21st March 1874, Ernest Pike was the third son of a respectable and well-known family. His father, Oliver had been a member of the Town Council, and of the Board of Guardians, the authority which locally administered the Poor Law Act. Even more significantly Oliver Pike was a Capital Burgess of Malmesbury, an honoured position within the Old Corporation of that town with origins dating back to Saxon times, to which men of substance, good character and social standing might aspire and be elected by their peers.

After an education at the Westport Boys National School Ernest dallied briefly with following his father into farming, but then joined the Army, from which his discharge was purchased after a short period of service. He joined the Wiltshire Constabulary on 28th November 1895 at the age of 21, being given the collar number of '7', and quickly justified school reports which with extraordinary prescience had characterised him as being intelligent but headstrong.

Plate d. Ernest Pike

Just before the end of 1897 he was noted for "great zeal, determination and pluck" in chasing and capturing George Parker, a young man of 20 who had committed highway robbery with violence at Somerford, relieving one Arthur Mashell of £6:10 shillings in gold. A desperate struggle ensued during which the criminal kicked Ernest in the testicles, but the constable nevertheless carried through the apprehension. Parker was brought up at the Wiltshire Winter Assize on 9th January 1898, and pleaded guilty to the charges. The Hon H.L. Lopes, prosecuting, asked the judge to reward Pike with something more than praise, and Mr Justice Bigham responded. Ernest got £5, and George got 12 months hard labour. The promising young constable was also rewarded by his Chief Constable with accelerated advancement to First Class Constable.

In 1898 he earned another commendation for good work during the annual military manoeuvres which involved the county force in an enormous amount of tough work. At the end of that year though, he showed the other side of his mercurial character when he was charged with parading for duty whilst under the influence of alcohol. Drink-related offences were then very common in the police, and apart from being tipsy on parade, Ernest does not seem to have compounded the sin by any associated acts of misbehaviour and the then Chief Constable, Captain Robert Sterne merely admonished him.

On 4th August 1903 he gained the grade and stripe of Merit Class constable, the last stage before promotion to sergeant.

That Glass of Beer
Burbage 21st May 1904

In 1902 Ernest had been posted to the country town of Burbage and two years later he again showed his partiality for a tipple when he called at the back door of a large house belonging to Mr J. Berveys in Grafton village. It was not uncommon for patrolling constables to call at private residences; in fact they were often required to do it and make a notebook entry which could subsequently be checked by a sergeant or inspector in order to confirm that patrols had been carried out as reported.

At night constables would slip a note through the letter box to confirm their presence without disturbing occupants. On this occasion though, Ernest was rewarded by a glass of beer provided by a servant. This turned out to be the most expensive drink ever taken in Wiltshire, for it led to a coincidental meeting which in turn was to be a direct cause, eight years later, of two policemen's deaths. This is how it started: Ernest's illicit refreshment stop at the Berveys house coming to the notice of his superiors, he was fined two day's pay and ordered to move station from Burbage before a posting would normally have been due for him.

The police took advantage of Ernest's unexpected sudden availability to fill a vacancy for a constable which just then happened to exist a few miles away in the village of Bottlesford between Devizes and Pewsey. This tiny settlement fell within the parish of Manningford Bohune whose souls were guarded by the vicar of nearby Wilsford,[28] the Reverend William Wrixon Keating, with whom Ernest became acquainted. Their friendship was to become the catalyst which would lead to the fatal finalé in 1913.

A Triumph for Ernest Pike
The Woodborough Station Incident 3rd November 1905

Within a matter of months of arriving at Bottlesford Ernest had shown his better side once more in a spectacular manner. The Great Western Railway line from the South West to Paddington ran through the nearby village of Woodborough, part of Ernest's patch, and on Wednesday 2nd November 1905 a break-in took place at the station there. Edward Shearing and William Patrick Donovan, two ne'er-do-wells from Bermondsey who had both been drummed out of the Army, had earlier tried to travel farther than their train tickets allowed, and were put back on to an east bound train at Savernake

---

[28] Wilsford (variously 'Willesford') near Pewsey, should not be confused with Wilsford-cum-Lake, a village which is located in the Avon valley south of Amesbury.

station near Marlborough. They got off at Woodborough to change trains, and whilst there they broke into the unmanned station office in order to steal cash. Finding none, they stole a portmanteau which had been left at the station, and after ransacking and discarding it a little way down the line, they returned to the station to make their escape back to London. Catching the next train, they may have thought as they steamed out of Woodborough that they had got away with their crime and that the local yokel bobbies were far behind them. They had not reckoned with Ernest Pike.

Hearing of the robbery, Ernest made what local inquiries he could, and gathered that the men hailed from London. The following morning he caught a Paddington bound train in pursuit of the two thieves, and by questioning staff at all stops, he found out that they had got off at Reading. Ernest then took to the Great West Road on foot, questioning members of the public and local policemen as he went. At Maidenhead the trail ran cold, so Ernest telegraphed a description of the men ahead and when he trudged into Slough some hours later he found that his foresight had been rewarded, for the police there had picked up the two men who were now waiting in the local nick.

Shearing and Donovan were so amazed at the Wiltshire bobby's persistence that they immediately confessed to the Woodborough robbery, and Ernest took them into his own charge, and returned with them to Devizes where they were locked up to await the pleasure of the magistrates who duly dealt with them some days later. Reward came eight months later when in July 1906 he was promoted to the rank of Sergeant (2nd Class) and posted to the Rodbourne Lane station in Swindon.[29] He obviously performed his duties well, being upgraded to 1st Class Sergeant on 17th November 1908. It would not have been unreasonable for him to hope for an inspectorship in due course.

---

[29] Boroughs with no independent forces were policed by their County Force in accordance with a formula based upon population at the date of the 1881 census, and by the time of the climax of the incidents covered by this book, April 1913, policing of the borough of Swindon was undertaken by 38 men of the 252-strong county force. See County Council Minutes – S.J.C., 24th April 1913. The 1911 Census shows that the ratio of policemen to the general population in Wiltshire was about 1:1000.

That Glass of Whisky
Swindon, 10th February 1909

But – and this seems predictable by now – he again strayed from the straight and narrow all too quickly, a glass of whisky causing his downfall this time. On 22nd February 1909 whilst on night duty Ernest called in at a police cricket club dinner. There he was offered food and a glass of Scotch, both of which he took. Being rather more used to ale, the unaccustomed spirits went quickly to his head, and later that evening he took it upon himself to interrupt a dinner being held at the Swindon Baths by the Borough Engineers Department. He was tipsy, but it seems that he was more embarrassing than offensive as he amused himself by repeatedly asking the guests whether they would like a cab. His idea of fun was not shared by the diners of course, and he was politely asked to leave. Unfortunately he refused to do so, only finally complying when a magistrate present at the time gave him the order to go.

Captain Llewellyn was now the Chief Constable, having assumed that position 10 months earlier and he clearly took a dim view of the incident which he felt, with some reason, brought great discredit on the Wiltshire Constabulary. Given Ernest's record of drink fuelled misbehaviour, it now seemed as though dismissal from the force was a definite possibility and he pleaded with Llewellyn for another chance to redeem himself. The Swindon Superintendent, an ex-Grenadier Guards' sergeant called Thomas Robinson who, since 1905, had also held the appointment of Deputy Chief Constable, made a written plea on Ernest's behalf. The comparatively lenient punishment awarded by Llewellyn was that Ernest be reduced to the rank and grade of first class constable and be posted, at his own expense, to the village of Enford. A vacancy had existed there for eight months since P.C. Cripps had been promoted and posted. Once again Ernest had been moved early for disciplinary reasons, this time with the added disgrace of demotion.

And so to Enford
February 1909

With Ernest and his family at Enford, and the new Chief Constable in post, the scene is almost set for the final *dénouement*, for Reverend William Keating was back in the picture, his parish being only a couple of miles from Enford. With sinister inevitability an explosive mixture of personalities was starting to assemble in and around the little village on the Avon, although it was to be nearly four years before the arrival of one more person ignited the fuse. We have to move through those years, but before we do, we must look back almost a decade to an incident which might provide a clue as to why Superintendent Robinson felt it necessary to support Pike in 1909. Could part of the answer lie in what had occurred at Salisbury Races in 1901?

The Race Plain Affair
May 1901 – May 1902

At the beginning of the new century Ernest Pike was a constable serving at Swindon, with a good record marked by two commendations, marred only by one minor disciplinary offence for which he had been admonished. He was occupying a cushy billet, being employed as groom to his divisional superintendent, Thomas Robinson.

In May of 1901 a 10-man detachment was sent from Swindon to help in the policing of Salisbury Races, and it was here that Ernest became the principal player in a notorious but now forgotten incident.

Salisbury Racecourse
Thursday 23rd May 1901

The Races opened on 23rd May 1901 on the course near the city generally known as 'The Race Plain'. In those days special trains came from London and elsewhere, and a strong police presence was always called for. It is interesting to note from the Constabulary Order Books which survive, that arrangements were always made for police firearms to be available, though whether this was necessary for veterinary euthanasia or for ultimate crowd control is not clear.

The detachment from Swindon was under the command of Superintendent Robinson, and it seems that the men enjoyed these duties. They received a few shillings additional pay from the organisers of the meeting, their evenings were free after the end of racing, and they were billeted in hostelries and inns in Salisbury, where no doubt the extra pay helped brewery profits.

On the first day of the meeting, a butcher named Eustace Wyndham Green, from the village of Sutton Mandeville near Tisbury a few miles east of Salisbury travelled to the Race Plain with his friend, Walter Gatehouse a traveller (sales representative) for Matthews Brewery of Gillingham, Dorset. They were obviously 'out for the day' as their little horse-drawn trap contained three one-gallon jars of beer and cider along with a good supply of food, but it certainly turned out to be unfortunate for them that they bumped into a policeman named John Alfred Dowling, with whom Gatehouse was acquainted.

At first all was well. Dowling, normally stationed in Wroughton, was part of the Swindon detachment, and was quite happy to accept his friend's offer to sample the contents of the stone jars, enjoying it so much that he invited his colleague Ernest Pike to join in, an invitation quickly accepted. *"We always chance our arms at Race Meetings"*, said Dowling some time later, to explain why the two men seemed to have little concern about drinking on duty in a public place. As they drank, the talk turned to the chances of horses in the day's events, and Pike fancied that a flutter on the mare '*Jettatura*' would be a likely investment in the first race on the card. The constables' bravado did not extend to being seen to be placing bets, and so they agreed with Gatehouse that if they gave him their stakes, he would put them on the fancied beast and collect any winnings on their behalf. Pike handed over half-a-crown (12½ pence), and Dowling two shillings (10 pence) and the men agreed to meet again by the Course Judge's box after the first race. Pike's eye for a nag was confirmed as Jettatura obliged by coming home first at odds of 5/1.

Unfortunately the meeting at the Judge's Box did not take place as planned, for the bookies selected by Gatehouse had fled the course without paying winnings, making threats of violence to disgruntled punters. At the end of the day's racing Dowling and Pike found Gatehouse, and heated words were being exchanged when butcher Eustace Green appeared again, and for some reason Pike decided to concentrate his ire upon him.

Almost immediately he accused Green of being a '*bloody welcher*' and struck him a violent blow in the face which sent the unfortunate man tumbling into a gorse bush. As the butcher attempted to stand, Pike struck another blow, and Green looked about him for assistance from Constable Dowling or from his friend Gatehouse, or from other constables nearby. None was forthcoming from any quarter, in fact Pike was being encouraged by other policemen who urged him to "*Give it to the bastard*" and so Green got to his feet and ran for the cover of a nearby wood. As he did so he was struck at again by another constable named Hutchings and a small posse of half a dozen policemen then chased him across open ground but he managed to lose his pursuers in the wood.

Pike now turned his attentions to Gatehouse, and demanded the amount of his winnings on pain of similar treatment as had been administered to Green. Now, Pike would have won twelve shillings and sixpence (62½ pence), and had his stake returned, making a total of fifteen shillings (75 pence) that he should have been paid, but be agreed to accept the sum of five shillings (25 pence) from Gatehouse, still a 100% mark up on his investment, and a further four shillings and sixpence (22½ pence) for Dowling. Gatehouse wisely paid him these amounts, and seemed to consider the matter settled, but Pike was still seething, and even whilst sitting in the horse drawn police brake that was taking the detachment back to their lodgings, he was loudly threatening to "*Get out and give the bastard another hiding*".

It was later alleged that the whole incident had been jocularly retold amongst the Swindon policemen in the bar at their lodgings in the Swan Inn at Harnham near Salisbury that night, a policeman named Payne reporting the conversation some months later.

Green emerged from hiding in the wood and met up with Gatehouse again near their trap. Both men then tried to find a Superintendent named Longstone, whom they knew to be present that day, but they were unsuccessful, Longstone probably finding it expedient to make himself scarce.[30]

Initial Inquiry, Salisbury Racecourse
Friday 24th May 1901

It was Gatehouse, not the assaulted Green who precipitated matters further, reporting the business to his village police sergeant some time during the Thursday evening, who in turn passed on the information to Superintendent Charles Fox of the Tisbury Division by 9.15 p.m. The following morning Fox called upon Green at his business premises in Sutton Mandeville, and from his quick inspection of the butcher's injuries he could see that some form of injury consistent with the allegation had obviously occurred, the man's lip being cut and bruised with another mark on the outside of the jaw. This was clearly a matter which required resolution, for if the accusation was true it was not only a nasty case of assault and battery, but was also a disgraceful breach of trust and police discipline. If it was not true, then it was an accusation that needed refuting, and so Superintendent Fox asked both Green and Gatehouse to accompany him to the Race Plain where he expected that day, to find the Chief Constable of Wiltshire, Captain Robert Sterne.

Sterne was indeed present, but his first action was not at all what Fox had anticipated, for the Captain berated the Superintendent for having left his divisional area in order to bring the men to the course. Fox persisted though, and Sterne agreed to look at Green's injuries, taking him to the flap of the police tent in order to do so. Fox was made to stand outside the tent whilst the Chief Constable questioned Green. Sterne declared that he could see no injuries, despite Fox and several others later testifying on oath that cuts and bruises were clearly visible

---

[30] Longstone very nearly achieved the considerable feat of serving under all of the first three Chief Constables, joining the force under Meredith in the 1860s. He retired less than a week before Llewellyn was appointed in 1908.

at the time and were still to be seen a week later. Despite his inability to see what was obvious to dozens of other witnesses, the Chief nevertheless ordered an identity parade which Pike at first managed to avoid attending, though Dowling was picked out. The absence of some men was noted, and when a full parade was held, Green picked out Pike as the man who had assaulted him. Pike immediately and categorically denied assaulting Green, but betrayed his aggressive intent towards the bruised butcher by unnecessarily adding: "..... *if I had hit you, I should have knocked your bloody head off*".

Swept under the Carpet
July – September 1901

A statement of the whole affair was then lodged with the police. The Chief Constable had shown that he was disinclined to act, but details of the assault had become known by certain magistrates and members of the Standing Joint Committee, at least one of whom, an elected member named Walker, attempted to press the matter at their next meeting on Thursday 24th July. The press were excluded from discussion of the matter, and no action was taken.

At the next meeting, three months later on 23rd October Mr Walker persisted, and put down a motion that Chief Constable Sterne should be given instructions to lay before the committee details of the complaint made by Gatehouse to Superintendent Fox. Although he had widespread support from members of the public, Walker was ploughing a lonely furrow in committee. The Chairman, Sir Godfrey Lushington, immediately stated, to a resounding *"Hear, Hear"* that any matters relating to the Chief Constable should not be discussed in public. Before going into conclave Mr Erlysman Pinckney J.P. let everybody know where the majority of the committee stood. There was only one receptacle for complaints like this he said – the waste bin! Why, he himself had consigned many there! Small wonder then that comment like the following should appear in the press:

"It is remarkable that when anything transpires at the meetings of the Standing Joint Committee to the credit of the police it is stated openly, but when there

is anything tending to the discredit of the force or any member of it the reporters are asked to withdraw and publicity is shunned. This created a very uneasy feeling, and in many quarters the conviction is growing that police administration in Wiltshire is far from what it should be."[31]

Quite unbelievably the Committee emerged from their closed session and announced that they were going to take no action. *"If Mr Green has a case"*, they said, *"then he has a remedy in the courts"*. The minutes of the meeting show that an amended motion proposing that a sub-committee be formed to look into the affair had been placed by Walker, but found no support. For forms sake it had been formally seconded so that it could be voted upon: the count was thirteen to one against. The suggestion by the County Justices who formed much of the S.J.C. that Green might like to take the case to law must have seemed like a taunt to Green, for the matter would come before their compatriots – maybe even them personally on the County Bench.[32] Fortunately he had some mettle.

County Sessions of the Peace, Salisbury, Tuesday 12th November 1901

Green, with support from a cross section of the community pursued the matter with the result that Ernest Pike was summoned to appear before the County Magistrates on Tuesday 12th November 1901 charged under the Offences Against the Person Act of 1861 with assault and battery, a misdemeanour which could be heard by the Justices sitting without a jury. Pike pleaded not guilty, and was defended by Mr Titley, a Bath solicitor who represented the police in many cases over many years. The prosecution was led by Mr Trevor Davies, solicitor of Yeovil. Trevor Davies obviously saw that the delay between the commission of the alleged offence and the issuing of a summons might be a problem, for he lost no time in making it quite clear that the delay had only occurred because Green had not wanted to initiate any prosecution until either the Chief Constable or the

---

[31] Salisbury and Wilton Times, 26th October 1901.

[32] The Racecourse lay outside the City boundaries, and therefore jurisdiction lay with county magistrates, not the separate city bench.

Standing Joint Committee had a chance to take internal disciplinary action against Pike. The S.J.C., which only met quarterly, had procrastinated at their July meeting and not disposed of the matter until the next meeting in late October.

Green and Gatehouse recounted their story, which was corroborated by a man called Tom Evans, a hotel keeper from Newport in Monmouthshire (now Gwent) who happened to be a relative of Gatehouse. Evans had been standing within five yards when the assault took place, and he positively identified Pike as the assailant. Captain Sterne stated that he had examined Green's face, but could not discover any sign of assault. Pike admitted drinking and betting, but absolutely denied assaulting Green.

So far all the evidence had been predictable. Then came an absolute bombshell of a witness. This was John Dowling, the friend of Gatehouse and fellow constable and betting partner of Pike. It transpired that he had resigned from the police on 1st September (he now worked for the Great Western Railway Company in Swindon) and now wished to tell a totally different story to that which he had officially reported in May.

He had left the police after a minor incident in which he had been accused of failing to keep a conference point, a charge he said he could show to be false and in a statement which was to be eerily echoed eleven years later, he said that he had not been allowed to bring his own witnesses and that his request for an inquiry was disregarded.

As Dowling had left the police under a cloud, it is not surprising that Pike's defence sought to discredit him as a witness, but it is worth noting two things when deciding whether the ex-bobby was simply out to make trouble. First, he was an experienced policeman, having served for nine years in the Metropolitan Force before coming to Wiltshire. Secondly, the unfair treatment which he claimed to have been subjected to was mirrored, albeit more delicately, in the case of Superintendent Fox, the senior officer from Tisbury who had been berated for taking Green and Gatehouse to see the Chief Constable.

Fox had enjoyed a blameless career, and was next in line in the county for promotion to 1st Class Superintendent. However, he was soon to retire early as his life in the force was made, in his own words, "*uncomfortable*", after he had become involved as a witness for Green.

Dowling totally corroborated the prosecution evidence in every respect. The testimony of a witness who '*turns Kings Evidence*' is rightly treated with caution, as it is usually the seedy and treacherous evidence of a culpable person who wishes to escape the full rigours of penalties which might otherwise attach to his conduct, by testifying against his former accomplices.

But Dowling was not quite in this position. No charge had been made against him, and so by coming forward and giving evidence he was not getting himself off any hook, but was actually implicating himself in crimes for his failure to come to Green's aid, and complicity in a conspiracy to cover up the incident. Not only did Dowling 'shop' Pike over the assault, but he went far further, disclosing three-way collusion between himself, Pike, and Superintendent Robinson to submit false reports of the matter. Dowling explained that shortly after the Race Plain incident, when back at his normal station in Wroughton, he had been called to Divisional Headquarters in Swindon to make his report about the matter. He bumped into Pike at the back of the station, who said to him,

"*We look like getting the bloody sack over this matter, but it's all right as long as we ain't summoned.*"

This suggests very strongly that Pike knew the police and S.J.C. would take no internal action, but that matters might be more perilous if court proceedings ensued. Pike then asked Dowling to make sure that their reports corroborated each other, supplying the Wroughton man with his own notebook to copy, remarking that such collusion had in fact been suggested by Superintendent Robinson. Dowling complied, and made out what he knew to be a false report which he handed to Robinson. Asked by counsel why he had allowed himself to become implicated in this fashion, Dowling said that things would have gone badly for him in the force if he had not done so, and that he felt bound to do what the Superintendent and Pike suggested:

"I told lie upon lie", declared Dowling, *"and I was bound to do it, that's a fact. That's the way things are in the Wiltshire Constabulary sir, that's a fact and I am a man of the world. But I am here today to speak the truth, and I will!"*

Whilst ready to admit that he had lied in his official report, he protected himself against more serious allegations by pointing out that the contents of his report were not given on oath,[33] but he did not spare the Swindon Superintendent, for he said that Robinson had told him that he knew all about the assault.

The defence, conducted by Mr Titley, who, like Pike and Robinson we shall meet again in 12 years' time, tried to discredit the prosecution witnesses, suggesting that there was a conspiracy to defame the police, though it might seem to any reasonably impartial observer that enough discredit had already been visited upon them by undisputed behaviour, for though he adamantly denied the accusation of assault, Pike admitted drinking and gambling whilst on duty and becoming involved in arguments with Green and Gatehouse. Strangely though, despite his admission to these self-confessed breaches of the police disciplinary code, he was never brought to account for them before the Chief Constable.

The evidence from Superintendent Fox, who at this point was still serving in the force, should have been convincing enough for anybody, as he had no prior cause whatsoever to be antipathetic to the police, but unfortunately his evidence directly contradicted that of Captain Robert Sterne R.N., Crimean War veteran, and Chief Constable of Wiltshire for the past 31 years. Fox quite clearly saw the injuries to Green's face. Sterne didn't, though the old sailor was careful to add that there were no injuries *"to the best of my belief."*

---

[33] Prior to the enactment of the 1911 Perjury Act the offence contravened only Common Law. A principal test was whether a statement was made on properly administered oath or affirmation. A false written statement in an official document was not then considered to be necessarily perjurious.

"Ah! To the best of your belief. I don't suppose you were very anxious to find them" said Mr Trevor Davies, in a remark which sums up what he, and many other people, suspected about the Chief Constable's evidence. Sterne confirmed that he had criticised Fox for going to the Race Course with the two aggrieved men, and that he had pointedly left the superintendent standing outside the police tent whilst he questioned Green and Gatehouse:

"Why?"

"Because I did not want his assistance at all," said Sterne.

Sterne then admitted having seen P.C. Payne's report about the boasting in the bar of the Swan, and said he believed it to a certain extent, *"because he himself, Sterne, had indeed seen a posse of constables pursuing a man, who he believed to be a 'welcher' to the woods"*.

In addition to calling a number of policemen, including Superintendent Robinson, to testify that they had seen nothing which would incriminate Pike, Mr Titley for the defence stuck to his strategy:

- *Why had the case not been brought immediately?* (We know: Green was trusting to the Standing Joint Committee and only proceeded when they failed to act.)

- *Why had Green and Gatehouse not made complaint to Robinson or Longstone at the course?* (They said they had tried, but could find neither. Pike was still railing, presumably within earshot, that he was going to administer another thrashing, and after being chased by a gang of police they perhaps felt a slight lack of confidence in any of the detachment still on duty at the course. They made complaint to policemen in their home village, where they presumably felt safe that very same evening though).

- *Was it not strange that the accusations had not been made until Dowling had left the police?* (Not so. The accusations had been laid before the Chief Constable immediately, and were before the Standing Joint Committee at their July meeting, Dowling did not leave the police until September).

- *Why had Green not obtained medical evidence of the injuries from a doctor?* (This would undoubtedly have been a wise thing to do, but although Titley's criticism was directed at Green and Fox, Sterne was also at fault in this respect).

- *The prosecution witnesses were all tainted in some way*, said Mr Titley. *Gatehouse was a friend of Green, Evans was a relative of Gatehouse. Dowling was a disaffected former member of the police.* (Titley did not mention Fox. There was nothing 'tainted' about his evidence, and at this point in time he had not yet shown any 'disaffection' by resigning).

In his own evidence, Ernest Pike suggested that Dowling "*had his knife into the Swindon men*" and he also made a curious remark about Fox. During cross-examination Mr Trevor Davies asked Pike if he was suggesting that Green's injuries were all a figment of Fox's imagination, to which Pike replied conspiratorially "*There's a lot in that, Sir!*" The prosecuting solicitor did not follow up on this comment, nor did he seem to make enough of hesitancy shown by Pike when he was asked about the contents of P.C. Payne's report of the conversation in the bar of the '*Swan*'. Trevor Davies seems though, to have lost his temper with Ernest over the matter of Dowling's report when Pike admitted handing his own notebook over to the Wroughton constable. Sight of it was required by Dowling, at Robinson's instigation, to ensure that the two men's reports complemented each other but when asked to say why he thought Dowling should need it, Pike could not admit any suggestion of collusion of course, and had to feign ignorance.

"*Are you so simple*" exploded the solicitor from Yeovil, "*that you could not understand what he wanted a copy of your report for?*"

Ernest Pike was very far from being a simpleton, so it must be the case that Trevor Davies' rude outburst was prompted by frustration at the constable contriving to avoid answering the awkward questions.

After all the evidence had been heard in what were undoubtedly tense and unpleasant proceedings, the time came for the Bench to retire and consider their findings. Would they be satisfied beyond reasonable doubt, as was required, that a crime had been committed?

Returning to court, the Bench dismissed the charge. There was, they said, insufficient evidence to convict, and Ernest Pike was therefore found not guilty.

Another round to Pike then, but Green, the man in the black and blue corner was by no means finished. He was still determined to bring Pike to justice, and he was not ploughing a lonely furrow for accounts indicate that he had a considerable amount of support amongst the local populace and press. The aggrieved man felt, no doubt, that in a case involving accusations against the police, the ancient English safeguard of trial by twelve good men and true was far preferable to one by a bench of County Magistrates. But a number of obstacles stood in the way. One was how to bring the case back into court after a finding of 'Not Guilty' had been handed down, for no man could be tried twice for the same offence, and a second was, if one tribunal had not been overwhelmingly convinced of Pike's guilt, what needed to be done to convince another? And thirdly, would not a new charge come before the same county magistrates who had shown that they were reluctant to find against a policeman who had the support of his Chief Constable?

The neat solution to these problems was to proceed with a new charge alleging another offence, perjury. Although County Justices might technically hear almost any case in Quarter Sessions, it was usual for the most serious matters to be reserved for the Assizes, but in cases of perjury there wasn't even a choice: trial by jury at the Assizes was mandatory. There was the matter of a preliminary hearing before magistrates to decide whether the case should go to trial, but part of the beauty of the solution was that these would not be the hostile county magistrates, for the alleged act of perjury had taken place within the jurisdiction of the Salisbury City Magistrates. Everything fitted: it must have seemed to the battered butcher as though things were starting to go right.

Salisbury City Magistrates Court
Thursday 13th February to Saturday 15th February 1902

Three months had elapsed since the protagonists had last faced each other in court, time enough for both sides to prepare their cases. The court room in Salisbury's Guildhall was full, crowds packing the floor and gallery, when the Aldermen of the City took their places on the Bench, led by the Mayor, Mr J.A. Folliott in full robes.

For the prosecution: Trevor Davies again.

For Ernest Pike, Titley had instructed a barrister named Metcalfe.

It is a measure of the public concern aroused by the whole Race Plain Affair that Trevor Davies in opening felt the need to deny any personal feelings in the matter. He gave a résumé of the November hearing, and informed the court that after the unsatisfactory result, his client (Green) had considered it his duty to search out further witnesses who would satisfy another tribunal that lies had been deliberately told in court. He also drew attention to the negative nature of the defence evidence, which he pointed out was hardly good testimony; it was always easy to find somebody who had seen nothing. He asked the Bench to dispose of the case by sending it for trial by jury.

Mr Metcalfe, for Pike, could not agree of course. He attacked the whole idea of a trial taking place at all. The device of substituting a charge of perjury for that of assault was, he said, no more than a confection intended to overcome the principle that no man could be tried twice for the same offence, for all the evidence to be submitted in this case would essentially be the same as that in the assault trial. He drew attention to an 1898 case at Flint Assizes which provided a precedent, he thought, for the magistrates to follow, and they should dismiss the present matter forthwith.

Oh, no, said Mr Trevor Davies. The principle of *autrefois acquit* (formerly acquitted) to which his learned friend was referring was a matter of some legal complexity, and certainly not one that should be dealt with by the City Bench (Mr T-D obviously did not believe in flattery as a device). The new charge, he pointed out, was in relation to a new offence, perjury, which had not been committed until Ernest Pike had taken the witness box under oath in November.

"*Proceed!*" said the Salisbury City Magistrates.

The first witness gave simple evidence, but it was an important element in any perjury trial. Francis Hodding, Clerk to the County Bench told the court that Pike had given his evidence in November, sworn on oath, that he had denied assaulting Green, and had been acquitted on the charge. This is a matter of some interest, because the right of an accused to give evidence was a recent innovation, having been introduced under the terms of the 1898 Criminal Evidence Act, prior to which an accused person was not considered to be a competent witness. It was Pike's decision to take to the witness box under oath – on Titley's advice no doubt – which opened him up to a charge of perjury.

After some brief technical matters had been dealt with, Eustace Wyndham Green was called to recount the same familiar story, which was repeated in essential detail by Walter Gatehouse who followed Green to the witness box. In cross-examination Mr Metcalfe took a similar line to that which Titley had taken in the earlier trial, attempting to undermine the credibility of prosecution witnesses. He asked Gatehouse if he had ever been convicted of any offence. When this sort of question is asked in court, it is usually rhetorical, the questioner knowing full well what the answer will be, and Gatehouse was forced to admit to a conviction in 1888 when he had been found to be in possession of stolen goods. Trevor Davies objected to the way in which Metcalfe approached this matter, and the mood of the public is shown by the fact that the intervention drew substantial applause.

Superintendent Fox added to his earlier evidence that the injuries to Green's face (which the Chief Constable – to the best of his belief, remember – could not see on the morning following the attack) were still visible to him three days later.

Pike gave his familiar evidence, admitting the gambling and drinking, but totally denying assault. Once more he insinuated that there was some sort of conspiracy to "get" the Swindon police detachment.

Then came a procession of fresh witnesses for the prosecution who had either seen various elements of the incident or Green's injuries. These were countered by others for the defence who said that they had seen or heard nothing. The weary process lasted an extraordinary three days, before the Bench were able to retire and consider their findings. After the experience in November, nobody could be sure which way the matter would go, but the case lived up to its unfortunate reputation for sensation when the aldermen returned to their places, and the Mayor addressed the body of the Court. He said that:

"..... *the Bench had given every possible consideration to the case, and were of the opinion that Green was assaulted, but a majority of the magistrates considered that there was not sufficient evidence against Pike to justify a committal for trial.*"

In other words, though the court was now prepared to accept that Green had been attacked, the present proceedings were not for a charge of assault, and so there could be no further action for that offence. No, the present proceedings were for perjury, and on that charge there was not sufficient evidence to satisfy enough of the magistrates that the case should be committed for trial. It is impossible to understand what sort of mental gymnastics members of the Bench went through in order to justify a dismissal given their acceptance that an assault had occurred, for given all the corroborative evidence the obvious culprit must have been Pike, who must therefore have been telling lies when he denied it.

Where do we go from here?

A refusal by inquiring magistrates to commit an accused to stand trial is not an acquittal. As the law then stood, a prosecution instituted before examining magistrates which was not proceeded with had to be referred to the Director of Public Prosecutions.[34] Further proceedings were then still possible, but were a highly unusual course, so the rejection of Green's case by the Salisbury Bench was the end of the matter of the Crown versus Pike. But Green and his counsel had certainly foreseen things going against them and they had their plan prepared. As soon as the magistrates delivered their decision, Trevor Davies leapt to his feet and quoting the 1859 Vexatious Indictments Act informed the court that his client intended to prosecute privately. The matter would now be referred to a Grand Jury at the next Assize.

Grand Juries and Vexatious Indictments

Grand Juries finally disappeared from English jurisprudence in 1933, except in London and the county of Middlesex where they could still be convened until 1948 in respect of certain unusual cases originating abroad.[35] Consisting of between 12 and 23 men they would hear a summary of evidence, and decide whether there was a case to answer and so they had historically acted as a filter to prevent frivolous or weak cases from wasting a court's time.

The decline of their importance was a long process, significant milestones coming with the Indictable Offences Act of 1848 and their abolition at Quarter Sessions in 1923, but in 1902 they still had a significant part to play in the indictment process. If they found a *prima facie* case they would write on the back of the Bill of Indictment '*True Bill*', which was the authority upon which the case might then proceed before a judge and 12-man Petty Jury.

Alternatively they might decide there was no case to answer and write '*No Bill*' and the matter would be taken no further. At least twelve Grand Jurors had to agree for a verdict to be reached, so this meant anything from unanimity to a simple majority depending on the number of Jurors empanelled. By the end of the nineteenth century Assize Grand Juries were not selected from a random cross section of eligible persons: it had become normal for them to be solely comprised of county magistrates.

[34] Prosecution of Offences Act 1879s 5
[35] Administration of Justice (Misc. Provisions) Act 1933 and Criminal Justice Act 1948, s2

Under Common Law, any person might submit a charge to a Grand Jury (this was known as a 'voluntary' bill), but by the middle of the nineteenth century there was seen to be a need for some sort of control and the Vexatious Indictments Act of 1859 imposed restrictions upon the right to charge certain offences, of which perjury was one. By bringing his case first before a lower court though, Green had fulfilled one important requirement of the 1859 Act. By then agreeing to be bound over to prosecute he fulfilled the other and was fully entitled to proceed with his private prosecution for perjury.

Wiltshire Summer Assize, Salisbury
Friday 30th May 1902

The Wiltshire Summer Assize opened on Friday 30th May 1902, a year and seven days after the assault on Green had taken place, His Honour Sir Thomas Townsend Bucknill presiding. One of the advantages of the Assize system was held out to be that visiting High Court judges were more likely to be immune to local pressures and prejudices, but 'Tommy' Bucknill, who had been a courageous amateur jump jockey in his youth, and had been Conservative Member of Parliament for Epsom from 1892 until 1899, had obviously heard about the Pike business, and far from bringing an impartial view he showed prejudice against the complaint even before it came into court. In his Charge to the Grand Jury he said that he had carefully read the depositions lodged with the court, and that he was surprised that complaint had not been made until November about an alleged assault in May. That red herring again! But things got worse; he then proceeded to remind the jurymen that the County Bench had delivered an acquittal in the matter, a fact that he was sure, he said, that the Grand Jury would consider very carefully. He, of course, would express no opinion, he sanctimoniously said, as he did not know enough of the case, but they should be very careful before they found True Bill in a matter which had been investigated by a proper tribunal, which had taken it upon itself to say 'Not Guilty'. This was a distortion, for the acquittal by the County Magistrates had been on the assault charge, not the perjury which was now alleged. But this partiality was typical of the approach of the judge to the entire business. In the other cases in the court calendar, Bucknill went on to tell the twenty three Grand Jurors, they had only to satisfy themselves whether there was sufficient evidence to justify trial, but perhaps, he said, they would go more minutely into the Pike case and satisfy themselves whether there should be a further prosecution. Of the seven County Magistrates who had heard the assault case in November, four were now members of the Grand Jury but if Judge Bucknill had consequently hoped for a receptive audience for his words, he was to be disappointed. They took the Pike case under scrutiny quite late on the Friday afternoon, and unexpectedly called for a number of witnesses to come before them, Green, Superintendent Robinson and Superintendent Fox all traipsing into the Grand Jury Room on the first floor of the Salisbury Guildhall. After a retirement of several hours they returned *True Bill*. Ernest Pike would take his trial by jury.

The case opened promptly next morning, Saturday 31st May 1902, and there were many familiar faces in court. Trevor Davies was there, having instructed Mr (later Sir) Arthur Clavell Salter, barrister, whose junior was Mr Holman Gregory. Pike's side had ratcheted things up too, and he was represented by a King's Counsel named Foote, who was accompanied by Mr Metcalfe. Mr Salter opened the prosecution by promising to prove to any reasonable man that Pike had told lies under oath. He would bring six witnesses to testify to the assault he said.

The defence line was quickly revealed. Foote K.C. described the attempt to prosecute Pike for perjury as a legal experiment which ought not to be allowed to proceed, as the evidence to be presented (with one or two trivial exceptions) was essentially the same as that given in the assault case. Bucknill had already made his own opinion on this point quite clear in his charge to the Grand Jury, and Mr Foote must have felt that he was on good ground for he felt confident enough to criticise the Grand Jury's decision. Obviously looking for a loophole, Judge Bucknill asked Mr Foote if he knew of any case where a judge had refused to allow a case to proceed after a grand jury had found a true bill, but Foote had to confess that he did not, and so the judge then said that he must allow the case to go on, though, he said, "*I have a strong feeling about it.*" That much was already obvious.

Salter, for the prosecution, seems to have been rightly alarmed by the early turn things seemed to be taking, and now said to the judge that whenever a summons was taken out, it must always be properly investigated. One might imagine that Bucknill could only agree to such a statement, but instead he replied enigmatically

"*There are cases and there are cases, Mr Salter.*"

Having attempted to persuade the Grand Jury to reject the case, and after unsuccessfully picking the defence's brains as to whether there was precedent which might allow him to stop it, the judge now tried his luck with the prosecution brief. Was there any chance, he asked Salter, of settling the case without continuing the trial? Salter's resolve now seemed to collapse, and he said that he would consult with Eustace Green. Solicitor Trevor Davies would undoubtedly have been party to the discussion, and although what the three said to each other is not known, the result was that Salter turned to Bucknill to say that he and Green felt that they must respect the very strongly expressed views of the learned judge and were now willing to withdraw the prosecution! Salter accepted responsibility for this course, which he admitted had been taken on his advice, and Judge Bucknill, clearly delighted, complimented Salter in condescending terms on taking the "right" course: "*Anyone who knew Mr Salter*", said Bucknill, "*would know that he knew how to pay attention to any observation from the Bench*", a worrying remark. Of course it was the judge's prerogative to stop the trial if he perceived a point of law which required it, but even the defence admitted that there did not seem to be such grounds.

The judge now spoke generously about Green and of the Grand Jury, in terms which have the air of great relief of a worried man who has suddenly seen opposition collapse. He advocated peace and harmony, and said that he hoped all those involved would shake hands and forget the past. The petty jury then returned a formal verdict of *"Not Guilty"* and the Salisbury Race Plain Affair of 1901/02 was at an end.

Charles Fox had prematurely retired from the police and now that the matter was no longer *sub judice* he wrote to the editors of all the newspapers in the county of Wiltshire stating that he thought that there had been a gross miscarriage of justice, powerful comment coming from a man who had been one of the senior policemen in the Shire. He also opened an appeal fund to cover Eustace Green's legal expenses. Fox's initiative was praised by the *Salisbury and Wilton Times*, which was less generous towards Bucknill, a judge who in the opinion of the newspaper had given in to his personal feeling, attempting to pacify rather than to judge. Both sides would have benefited from a full and final inquiry which jury trial would have provided, said the paper's editorial comment, going on to point out that suspicion remained firmly implanted in the minds of many citizens. To be fair to Bucknill, he did attempt to make it clear that his objections were based on points of law, not the facts of the case.

What are we to make of this business, and what relevance has it in the years leading up to the 1913 *finalé*?

The most damning evidence against Pike was Dowling's which should have decided the matter of guilt on the assault charge immediately.

The defence may have claimed that he was a disaffected witness, but his evidence, never shaken, was supported by Gatehouse. Here was direct evidence from two witnesses who saw everything, corroborated by circumstantial testimony from other witnesses which confirmed the allegations. Not the least of these was Superintendent Fox's, but even Chief Constable Sterne's defence evidence admission of seeing a police hue and cry also tended to confirm Green's story. Pike had stated in the assault hearing that he did not chase Green into the wood, *"an absolute lie"*, he called it, yet Sterne admitted that he saw a posse of constables chasing a 'welcher'.

Who else could the pursued man have been but Green? Even if by a generous stretch of the imagination we allow that such a chase involving someone else had occurred, and that Green and Gatehouse without any obvious motive worked it into an elaborate plot to discredit the police, all that would have been necessary to demolish the prosecution case was for the policemen involved in the chase seen by Sterne to be produced in court to say they had not been after Green.

Odd verdicts can occur in completely honest proceedings, but it is quite impossible, even now, to believe in Pike's innocence, and it seems very likely that he was helped by senior policemen, magistrates and a judge who were prepared to ignore the truth. Is this far-fetched? Would English police and courts behave in such a manner? It is a frequently observed fact that society often turns a blind eye to the rights of certain groups of people of whom it chooses not to approve. One only needs to think of the outcry when somebody uses excessive force against a criminal; the public approve, and the press castigates those who are obliged to investigate and deliver judgement along the lines that "It wouldn't have happened in the old days". In 1901 the gentlemen who sat on magistrates benches would have privately considered that Green and Gatehouse, having accepted Pike's stake, had a moral obligation to honour winnings regardless of any loss they might have incurred at the hands of others.

The magistrates would consider a welcher to be an unspeakable rogue, yet one against whom a complainant had no legal remedy. Horsewhipping would be in order, and the more earthy approach of a wronged constable would not worry them too much so long as the welcher got what he deserved. And furthermore, those were the days when magistrates and judges invariably treated policemen's evidence in court as though it were gospel truth, a situation which, broadly speaking, can be said to have continued until the middle of the twentieth century. Drawing a stark distinction between the standards of earlier times and those today, a prominent modern magistrate says this:

"Any indication that the magistracy is connected with, has obligations to, or administrative authority over the police or any other prosecuting body or official, dangerously undermines the public's belief in the independence and

impartiality of the Bench – ***a belief that is of recent origin*** *– and could easily be shattered."*[36] (Author's emphasis).

As for relevance to events in following years, it may be this: that Ernest Pike had drawn senior officers into a conspiracy which with their help had succeeded. Those who colluded with him would now be wary of his capacity to expose them as fellow perjurers. This may explain why he was leniently treated after his second and third disciplinary offences and why Robinson attempted to protect him after the 1909 Swindon Baths incident. By then though a new Chief was in place who would not be personally threatened by Pike's dangerous inside knowledge. So in 1909 when Pike was faced with the threat of dismissal with loss of pension rights, Robinson might have felt he had to help Pike to prevent him 'blowing the gaffe' in the way that Dowling had done after he left the police in 1901. On the other hand there would be other policemen who resented the way Pike got away with so much. Perhaps some of them thought that his come-uppance was long overdue.

In 1903 Mr Trevor Davies, the solicitors who represented Eustace Green, was forced to take County Court action for recovery of his fees and expenses. Trevor Davies claimed that he only took the case on the understanding that his fees would be guaranteed by Superintendent Fox.

Trevor Davies won an order against Green and Fox by which they were obliged to settle the debt in instalments.

It is tempting to speculate that the two men felt themselves to have been poorly served by their lawyers.

If Pike had sown a storm in 1902 when he benefited so much from the protection of his seniors, he would reap a bitter whirlwind in 1913.

---

[36] Alan Maddox LL.B, 'The Work of a Magistrate (5th Ed.). Shaw and Sons, 1994.

Chapter 4

The Cast Assembles

The Avon Valley, February 1909 – March 1913

Seven years after the end of the Race Plain affair, Ernest Pike, having been a sergeant for thirty months but now a constable once more, arrived in the village of Enford to be the sole representative there of the law. A small thatched cottage on a hillside overlooking All Saints Church was both home and police station to the constable and to his growing family. In 1899 Ernest had married Amelia "Millie" Hanks, a school mistress of Great Somerford, a village in the north of the county of Wiltshire near to his own home town. She was a daughter of a Malmesbury family, some members of which tenuously claimed relationship to Nancy Hanks of Virginia who was the mother of Abraham Lincoln.

Amelia had borne Ernest five children by the time the family arrived in Enford, and was to produce another boy two years later in 1911. The first three offspring were all girls. Their fourth child, James Ernest, had been born on 23rd February 1905 whilst the Pikes were living at Bottlesford, whence Pike had been posted after being found guilty of accepting the glass of ale from the servant in Burbage the previous May and little James was baptised in the nearby parish church of Manningford Bohune by the Reverend William Keating on the 9th April.

The Reverend William Wrixon Keating M.A.

Born in 1846 into a well-connected Anglo Irish family, Keating was the third son of Henry Keating of Mallow, Co. Cork. After graduating B.A. from Trinity College, Dublin in 1870 he was ordained at Cork, and served as deacon in a parish in Skibereen before moving to England and holding curacies at Linslade in Berkshire, Eton in Buckinghamshire, All Saints Torquay and St Johns, Surrey Road, Bournemouth. His priesthood was conferred by the Bishop of Oxford in 1874, and two years later he was granted his M.A. by T.C.D. In early 1881 we find him lodging at the house of a Mr John Coe at 28 Church Road, in the parish of St. Mary Magdalene at Hastings in Sussex and later that year he was appointed to the parish of St Nicholas's Wilsford, a living which had been within the patronage of the Master of St. Nicholas's Hospital, Salisbury since 1227.

The new vicar of Wilsford was striking in appearance and behaviour. A tall, fine figure of a man, even when well into his sixties, with long flowing hair and beard, he had a lively, even volatile, disposition. Blessed with an Irish love of fun, he was an amusing conversationalist, well equipped with anecdotes which he could deliver in a racy style. He had talent too, for he was known as a good singer who often performed at concerts in Devizes and the villages of the area. A lifelong bachelor he lived at Wilsford Vicarage with his mother, Mary Anne, who died at the age of 81 in August 1895, and in due course he saw to the installation of a stained glass memorial window to her which may still be seen in the north eastern part of his old parish church.

Though an Anglican, he seems to have had many of the traditional attributes of an Irish country priest, a devotion to his flock, and a readiness to vigorously correct or protect them. He was particularly concerned with the well-being of policemen of his acquaintance, not an unusual thing for a vicar at the time – policemen were, after all, representatives of stability and order and were a useful conduit of information to a parish priest. In the case of the Pike family though, the working relationship developed into personal friendship, unusual, almost scandalous in the way it transcended class boundaries. When Ernest's promotion to sergeant in 1906 resulted in a move to Swindon, Keating and the Pikes maintained contact.

In February 1909 when the family moved to Enford they found themselves to be only two or three miles from Keating's parish, and the clergyman immediately took to visiting, often sending Amelia and the children for rides in his governess cart whilst he stayed in the little home-cum-police station and talked with Ernest.

THE CAST ASSEMBLES

Now, although Ernest liked Enford he was upset by the circumstances which had brought him there, for rather than accepting that he had been leniently treated over the affair at Swindon Baths, he felt that he had been let down. He explained to Keating how he had called in at the Police Sports and Social Club at about 11.30 p.m. whilst on duty that night in February 1909 and had been given strong drink which affected him badly. He had made a fool of himself there was no denying that, but one of the officers encouraging him to accept the drink offered by an Inspector, he told Keating, was none other than his old boss Superintendent Robinson, who since 1905 had held the appointment of Deputy Chief Constable.

Ernest's version of the story was that Robinson advised him to plead guilty and promised to see that he wouldn't get into too much trouble. Ernest was consequently shocked to find himself posted and demoted and claimed that Robinson had not kept his word. After Ernest was dead Robinson denied ever making such a promise, but it is a matter of record that he did in fact put in a mitigating written report to the Chief Constable. Whether or not Pike knew of this, he still felt aggrieved that he had been led astray and then let down.

Keating was not the man to simply sit back and sympathise when he heard Pike's version of the narrative. He sought an interview with Llewellyn and over the space of an hour and a half he complained to him about the punishment meted out to Pike. A more perceptive man than the Wilsford vicar would have realised that he was only irritating the Chief Constable who had shown that he did not like outside interference by anybody, but Keating injudiciously pressed on and even named the inspector who had actually handed the whisky glass to Pike, to which Llewellyn replied protectively: "*It was Pike's fault for accepting the drink, not the inspector's for giving it!*" The clergyman then complained that he thought the Chief Constable's disciplinary regime was too harsh, and one can sense the Captain's anger from his terse reply – "*I learned it in the navy!*" Nevertheless Llewellyn remained courteous, and when Keating described his visits to the constable's family, said that he was: "*glad that he* (Keating) *was kind to the force and did not think of its men as machines.*"

Keating and Llewellyn were almost neighbours, living about two miles from each other in a rural area, and it is certain they met socially from time to time, as the Chief Constable later complained that the clergyman would raise the subject of Pike every time they met. Keating later said that after this interview in early 1909 he had not raised the question of Pike again for a further two years, although he made subsequent representations in respect of two other policemen with whom he was acquainted. When Keating eventually did speak again to the Chief Constable about Ernest in 1911, Llewellyn replied, *"Don't trouble. I am going to make him a sergeant again directly"*, with the result that the impetuous clergyman rushed to Enford and told Pike that he had better start packing, for he was soon to be promoted!

How serious the Chief Constable was in making his remark can never be known. To his credit, he had not at this point allowed Keating's interference to harm his view of Pike, who was certainly doing well in Enford. Although the sleepy village had not provided him with the opportunities to pull off the dramatic *coups* of the kind that had proved so useful to his career in the past, he was popular, efficient and well behaved, winning back his Merit Class grade in 1910. This was not simply a routine matter either, as there was a 25% limit on the number of constables on the county police establishment who could be graded as merit class. It is on record that on Christmas Eve 1912 he said that he had grown fond of Enford, and had no desire to return to town duty. He liked his neighbours and when his sergeant's name came up, he had nothing bad to say against Frank Crouch. He was, it seems, happy at Enford, at least until the end of the year 1912 when fate played another cruel hand and finally placed the last piece in the diabolical mosaic of personalities.

The Divisional Reorganisation, 12th November 1912

The idea of new police premises in Amesbury had first been raised with the S.J.C. in 1904, but was shelved because of cost. In 1909 a comment had been minuted by the S.J.C. that the old Amesbury station was *"not a credit"*, and that it was *"a disgrace that policemen should be put into such a place."* On 16th May 1913 a correspondent of the *Police Review* described conditions in his own station. Although he was writing from another county, his colourful words give some idea of what policemen had to put up with.

"I would like our Chief Constable's attention drawn to the insanitary condition of some of our police stations and parade yards. You can see about a dozen stray dogs fastened up in old soap boxes; they are continually howling, and create an awfully foul smell in damp weather. In the same yard are about 40 head of poultry using the yard for a hen run, the water closets for roosts and the ash pits for scratching grounds. It is impossible to walk across the yard without getting smirched with hen dung, and the effect upon the sewers and drains is obvious. It is impossible for men to keep in good health whilst living in such places."

Chief Constable Llewellyn raised the matter at a meeting on 15th July 1909, citing operational necessity. Soon after, as the Army started to station increasing numbers of personnel permanently in garrison areas north of Amesbury, the County Constabulary saw the need to strengthen their presence in the area,[37] and whilst it was a straightforward enough thing to simply station constables near the new military establishments, it was further felt that a proper administrative centre should be locally established.

The Chief Constable's concern prevailed, and a decision was taken not only to improve the station facilities in Amesbury, but to set up a new police division headquarters, taking over parts of the operational areas of the Devizes, Salisbury and Marlborough Divisions. In 1912 a splendid new police station was erected in the town by Westbury contractors Messrs Parsons at a cost of £5,700 in addition to the price of the land, an original plan to include a court room being abandoned. Tiled cells were attached, together with houses for the superintendent and sergeant, section house accommodation for three single constables, a coach house and stabling, and various other modern amenities. The premises were a little too grand for the liking of some folk, as witnessed by a

---
[37] Standing Joint Committee Minutes 2nd February 1912.

newspaper editorial of the time, referring to, "... *the positively palatial police premises which have been erected in Amesbury at a cost of between £5,000 and £6,000*". The report commented on, "*the magnificence of the new building which is the residence of the superintendent of the division, a sergeant, and some unmarried constables, together with de luxe accommodation for such surprised prisoners as may be fortunate enough to get locked up there.*" This was churlish comment, considering the bad condition of many police stations and houses.

Once the new building at Amesbury was ready for use the Chief Constable gave the order for the division to become operational on 12th November 1912.[38] Officers within its area were now administratively transferred, including P.C. Pike at Enford, and Sergeant Frank Crouch at Netheravon both of whom had previously been administered by Superintendent Alexander Mackie's Marlborough division. Inspector Archibald Buchanan was promoted to the rank of superintendent at the end of October and posted from Trowbridge to command at Amesbury, relieving Inspector Cowdry who was sent to Swindon, and with these routine movements came Ernest Pike's nemesis.

Almost immediately complaints about Pike's friendship with Keating started to be made from Amesbury Division to the Chief Constable, a situation unwittingly aggravated by the clergyman writing to Llewellyn on 4th January 1913 asking once again for Pike to be promoted when he next was moved. The source of the harassment was Archibald Buchanan, who now had direct power over Ernest Pike.

Why, though, should he have such a down on the Enford bobby? Jealousy may have played a part. Apart from Chief Constables, all police officers had risen through the ranks, and no matter what position of authority they achieved in the police, they could not, in those class conscious days, escape the fact of their humble origins. Buchanan, a native of Deal in Kent and only three months older than Ernest Pike, had been a carpenter before joining the police, and it might have galled

---

[38] Force General Order No.125 of 8th November 1912

him that he, despite his rank, could not establish friendships with 'the quality' in the way that Pike had done with the reverend gentleman.

This is more than simple speculation, for Pike himself would claim jealousy as a motive behind the harassment, but there is in fact a much more likely reason for Archibald Buchanan's attitude. Keating, primed by Pike, had tried to 'drop Buchanan in it', by naming him to the Chief Constable as the inspector who had given whisky to Ernest Pike at the police function in February 1909. Now, four years later, Buchanan was in a position to exact revenge and was very well placed to do it too. Not only was he Ernest's divisional commander, but his elder brother, Superintendent Robert Buchanan, was Llewellyn's Senior Administrative Officer ('Chief Clerk', in 1913 terminology), who, assisted by his son P.C. Robert Buchanan Jr, worked alongside the Chief Constable in the County Police Headquarters in the old Militia Barracks on Bath Road, Devizes. Archibald thus had a fraternal channel to the Chief Constable's ear, which he needed if he were to harm Ernest, for despite holding Superintendents rank he had no delegated disciplinary powers. What better way of harming him was there than by playing on Llewellyn's dislike of his men having 'outside' friendships?

Plate e. Archibald Buchanan

Keating had been bothering the Chief Constable for years, but there had been no particular focus on Pike; he was one of many on whose behalf the clergyman interjected. Llewellyn even seemed to approve of Keating's visits to the Pike family, but Archibald Buchanan quickly changed Llewellyn's perception of the relationship, and he gave the matter some priority, for despite only arriving in his new post on 12th November he nevertheless had a derogatory report about Pike's friendship with Keating on the Chief Constable's desk before November was out.

The Chief Constable, probably primed by Robert Buchanan, was susceptible to Archibald's views on Pike, and from now on would say quite openly that he saw it as his duty to break up the friendship with Keating. At the next available reorganisation of the dispositions of the force, Pike was warned for posting with effect from a date in April.[39] Although a general rotation was due and Pike could have expected to move in the normal course of events (hopefully with promotion) the reason for selecting Colerne for Pike's new station was, as Llewellyn later unashamedly admitted, for the express purpose of moving him as far away as possible from Keating.

On 1st March 1913, Ernest's immediate superior, Sergeant William Frank Crouch of Netheravon walked up to Enford to pass on the formal posting notification to Pike.

Police Sergeant Number 186, William Frank Crouch

Frank Crouch had arrived in Netheravon on 5th August 1909 as station sergeant just a few months after Pike had moved to Enford. He came from a family which had enthusiastically enlisted in the police, having relatives in the Wiltshire Constabulary, the Bath City force and also the Met. A married man with two young boys by the time he moved to Netheravon, Frank Crouch seems to have been a steady character in contrast to the mercurial Pike. An agricultural labourer before joining the police, the sergeant had never had a bad mark against him, but by the same token he had never excelled in any way sufficient to earn any sort of commendation. His unimaginative steadiness is perhaps best illustrated by his conduct in connection with a case which

---

[39] Force General Order No.128 dated 28th February 1913.

earned him a brief moment of fame when his photograph appeared in national newspapers.

The Burbage Well Murder

By chance, Ernest Pike's replacement at Burbage after his removal for drinking the glass of ale in May 1904 was Constable Frank Crouch. In July 1907, acting on information received, Frank discovered the decomposing body of a child in a well, but attempts at identification proved fruitless. The police failed to make any connection with the fact that Mary Ann Nash, a resident of Aughton only four miles away had explained the disappearance of her eleven-year old illegitimate son Stanley by saying that he had been sent to live with relatives.

Plate f. Frank Crouch

It took three and a half years for the penny to drop, but when it eventually did, in early 1911, Mary was brought to trial for murder. When Frank Crouch was placed in the stand to give his evidence he had to state that he no longer had his notebook containing his report of the discovery of the body. His grounds were that it was standard procedure to destroy notebooks after three years, and whilst this was correct, strictly speaking, the destruction of evidence relating to an unsolved death displayed a lamentable lack of initiative. Somehow one cannot imagine his predecessor at Burbage acting so thoughtlessly.

Frank was not alone though; the village doctor, a man named Farquhar, had also destroyed his own 1907 notes, but being fearful of the sort of criticism laid at Frank Crouch's door, he produced a new set from memory and presented these as original documents. He was rumbled, and as a result of his weakness he was convicted of perjury at the Wiltshire Summer Assizes in May 1911, but escaped imprisonment. His offence was particularly shameful, for he had concocted evidence simply to save himself from embarrassment in a case in which a woman was on trial for her life.

Mary Nash was found guilty of the murder of her son, and was sentenced to death, the execution being scheduled to take place at Devizes Gaol. She was reprieved.[40]

Their Last Month on Earth
March 1913

Pike's relationship with Crouch still seems to have been good and he took the news of his posting well enough. When the younger man had arrived in Netheravon on promotion as Pike's superior in 1909, the Enford constable congratulated him. "*You have got the stripes, and I hope that you will keep them.*" Ernest said to Frank Crouch, "*I had them once and lost them. It was through my own fault, and I must try to get them back again.*" Until March 1913 Crouch had no cause to find fault with Ernest and had seemed well disposed towards him. When duties attracting extra pay became available, Crouch would generally put these the way of Pike as an act of kindness, "*in view,*" as he put it once to his wife Alice (née Weston, of Devizes, usually known as Kate) "*of Pike's long family.*" The sergeant had been asked once in Devizes how Pike was getting along in Enford, to which he is said to have replied: "*Oh Pike is all right. He is doing very well and will soon have his stripes once again. I hope he does, for he deserves it.*" Crouch's duty visits to Enford were not matters for the village constable to fear, for the sergeant would often be seen receiving simple hospitality from the Pike family.

Things changed in March.

---

[40] Very few executions took place at Devizes. No woman was hanged anywhere in Britain between 1908 and 1921, although fifty-one were sentenced to death and reprieved during this period of Liberal government.

The Fuse Ignited.
The 'Three Horse Shoes' incident
10.30 pm Tuesday 4th March 1913

Three days after telling Ernest that he was to be transferred to Colerne, Frank Crouch paid an unexpected visit to Enford, this time late at night. He called at Pike's house, according to his own report, at 9.30 and asked Amelia where her husband was. "*Down the village,*" said the constable's wife. One account tells us that Crouch entered the house for a glass of ale, and although Crouch does not admit as much in his report this would explain why he did not arrive in the village centre until 10.00 p.m. as the walk from the little house would take only two or three minutes. Had he thought that he might catch Ernest in licensed premises, he certainly had a great deal of time in which he could have checked both public houses in the village, as *The Swan* and the *Three Horse Shoes* are within a few hundred yards of each other.

It was a very windy night so Crouch would have taken up a sheltered spot in which to stand, one which did not afford him the best of views, especially as it was dark, the third quarter waning moon unrisen before midnight. At 10.30 he heard the latch of the Three Horse Shoes door fall, and stepping into the road he saw Ernest Pike standing nearby.

"*Where did you come from?*" demanded the Sergeant.

"*From Chisenbury,*" said Pike, naming a hamlet a mile to the north which was part of his patch. "*I have been here five minutes.*" (It was quite normal for a constable to stand outside a public house at closing time).

"*You have not,*" said Crouch, indicating the pub, "*you have come from that house*".

Crouch then became aware of another presence near the pub door, and striking a match he espied Tom Phillimore, the son of the landlord, standing under the flapping canopy of the next door butchers shop. The young man had come outside in order to go around to the stables attached to the rear of the inn to help his father,

Walter, stable the horse which had just drawn him back from the village of Everleigh. It was most certainly Tom, not Ernest Pike, that Crouch had heard come through the doorway.

The young man, confronted by two arguing policeman seemed terrified, and Crouch had to speak to him three times before getting an answer. When Tom found his tongue he denied that Pike had been in the bar. Dissatisfied with this, Crouch asked where his father was. "*In the stable*", was the reply from Tom, who then called through the door to his mother, Emma: "*Here is the sergeant. He wants to see you.*" Mrs Phillimore was quite adamant that the village bobby had not been in her pub that night, and this was repeated by her husband who now came around from the stables.[41] Crouch then told Pike to account for his movements.

The sergeant's report was written up by the next morning, but Ernest had no need to submit a written report until he was informed that disciplinary action was going to be taken against him. The two accounts contain important differences. Ernest's is reproduced here because it is the more thorough.

"<u>Statement of duty done on Tuesday March 4th 1913, between the hours of 5 p.m. and 10.45 p.m.</u>

Sir, I have the honour to report that on Tuesday March 4th, I attended a meeting point at Chisenbury, 6 p.m. and conferred with P.C. Slade. I walked to Jenner's Farm in company with P.C. Slade, visited Compton, and returned to my station, 8 p.m. I left my station 8.15 p.m., and proceeded to Long Street, visited the Swan Inn, returned to Salisbury Road, visited New Town and Fifield and Coombe (returning to Long Street) 9.30 p.m. where I saw five or six persons leave the Swan Inn, one of them being John Spreadbury, who came up and spoke to me as I stood on the corner. I walked with him to the racing stables, where I wished him "Good Night" a going up Water Lane, and I proceeded along Littlecott to Chisenbury, arriving here at about 9.55 p.m. I stood under the wall by the Little Arch within sight of the Red Lion. Walter Phillimore, landlord of the Three Horse Shoes, Enford, passed me driving a horse and trap,

---

[41] Walter had probably arrived home at about 10.05 p.m.

THE CAST ASSEMBLES

Plate g. The Phillimore Family. Tom Phillimore is on the right. The blind under which he stood on the night of 4th March 1913 is behind him.

and wished me "Good-night." A strong S-W wind was blowing. About five minutes later another man passed whom I wished "Good-night," and he answered me. I waited till about 10.15 p.m.: no one turned out of the Red Lion, Chisenbury. I then walked back through Chisenbury to Littlecott House, the late residence of H.de H. Whatton Esq., but which is now closed, the furniture there awaiting sale. I walked around the house and tried the doors and found all right. I then proceeded towards Enford, arriving opposite the Three Horse Shoes about 10.20 p.m. I heard footsteps coming towards me I stood still, and Sergeant Crouch came up and asked me where I had been. I told him I had just come from Chisenbury. He replied, "Didn't I hear you come out of that house just now?" I said "Certainly not, Sergeant." He said, "I will know," and went across and knocked at the door, at the same time struck a match, which showed up Thos. Phillimore, the landlord's son, standing outside the door under the verandah. Sergeant Crouch said, "Why didn't you speak?" Mrs Phillimore came to the door, and Sergeant Crouch asked her if she had seen Pike tonight. She replied, "No, I have not seen him tonight". He then asked to see the landlord, and Phillimore came to the door with a hurricane

THE CAST ASSEMBLES

lantern in his hand. Sergeant Crouch asked him if Pike had been in tonight. He said, "No, sir. I have not seen him in the house tonight." Sergt Crouch and I then walked in the direction of Enford Hill. He asked me what time I went to supper, and I told him 8 p.m. He then asked me who I passed on the road coming from Chisenbury. I told him I only passed two men, both of whom I wished "Good-night": one answered me and the other one did not. He asked me who they were. I said I could not say, as it was too dark and a very rough wind. I also told him that Walter Phillimore passed me driving a horse and trap with both lamps lit about 10 p.m. He replied, "I was on the corner at 10 p.m. and I saw no horse and trap return to Phillimore's". I said, "I hope you will go and ask him." He then asked me if I was going to Colerne tomorrow, I said "I can't go if it is weather like this, but if it is fine I intend going". He said, "Book me at 10.45 p.m., Littlecott". That was the time then, and we were standing on the top of Enford Hill. – I have the honour to be Sir, Your Obedient Servant, ERNEST PIKE P.C. 7"

(N.B. 'Little Arch', Pike's observation point near the Chisenbury Red Lion, is a spot where a stream flows under the road and wall about fifty yards from the door of the Red Lion. The time he claims to have arrived there, 9.55 p.m., fits well with the undisputed time he bade good night to John Spreadbury. However, he could not possibly have left there at 10.15 and arrived in Enford on foot at 10.20 p.m., and he would not have knowingly claimed to do so. No comment was made about this at the time, so it must be assumed that a reporting or printing error has occurred. He most probably left Chisenbury immediately after the Red Lion closing time).

Differences in the two men's accounts are these:

Crouch's report said that Ernest claimed to have been standing by the Three Horse Shoes for 5 minutes before the sergeant approached him, and yet in Ernest's written report he claimed to have just arrived. Much was later made of the fact that Crouch says that he did not hear Pike arriving down the flint road in his hard boots, a fact which might be easily explained if Pike had in fact been standing still in the shadows for 5 minutes.

Ernest wrote that Crouch said that he had been "*on the corner*" at 10 p.m. The Sergeant in his own report only reported leaving the Enford police house at that time.[42] It is only about 150 downhill yards from the house to the corner of Enford Hill and Longstreet, say a two minute walk, but the exact times that the two men claimed to have been in particular positions was important. It is understandable that any significance in these seemingly trivial details was overlooked at first, but once charges were made their importance should have been clear to any impartial investigator.

Most important of all though is the fact that there is no mention in Crouch's report of any claim by Pike to have seen Walter Phillimore at Chisenbury, though Ernest's report submitted a week later says that he did mention it to the sergeant, an anomaly which would acquire later significance.

Wednesday 5th March 1913

On the morning after the confrontation in Enford Crouch made his initial report to the Superintendent. There seems little doubt that it provided Buchanan with the opportunity he had been waiting for, and which might yet elude him if Pike escaped his clutches by moving to Colerne. He lost no time in calling for Walter Phillimore to come to Amesbury. There is no doubt that the landlord told Buchanan that Pike had not been in the Three Horse Shoes, but whether he told him that he had seen the constable at Chisenbury at 9.55 p.m. would later become an important question. Phillimore had indeed been to Everleigh, so Crouch's comment to Pike that he had not seen the landlord return in the trap can only cast doubt on the sergeant's account of what he saw. Either he *had* seen him and was lying, or he was telling the truth which means that he was not well enough placed

---

[42] Crouch reported that he called at the Pike's house at 9.30 p.m. At this time Pike was seen "standing on the corner" by five or six men who were leaving the Swan. Four would provide written statements supporting his story. If Crouch had gone immediately to the village after calling at Pike's house, he would probably have met Pike there. In view of the accusations against Pike, it would indeed be ironic if this meeting did not occur because Crouch had been supping Pike's ale. 'The Corner' was probably the junction of Enford Hill and Longstreet, from where a good view of much of the village centre can be gained. From here the Three Horse Shoes and The Swan can be observed - as long as the light is good.

to see and hear a lighted, steel tired, horse drawn vehicle. In that case, how could he possibly have insisted that he would definitely have heard a man on foot over the same stretch of road?

Did Buchanan query the obvious weaknesses in the sergeant's report of the incident? He should have done, but his own written words will help us to see again and again that the superintendent did not want to hear evidence for Pike. All he is recorded as saying to Phillimore at the time is "*I would rather believe the sergeant than you. If Pike did not come out of your house then he must have come down from the clouds.*" But Buchanan had not finished his work, for he now forwarded Crouch's report to Llewellyn with the first of a series of spiteful covering letters.

"*Sir - I have the honour to forward this report from Sergt. Crouch against P.C. Pike for your information. I have interviewed the landlord myself, but he states that Pike was not in the house, but Pike could not have come down the road from Chisenbury without Sergt. Crouch hearing him, as there are a lot of new stones down. Also, Pike states he was in Chisenbury at 7 p.m.; he had no cause to go there again at 10 p.m. The landlord and landlady no doubt are afraid they will get into trouble. Pike also states he met two men on the road, and did not know who they were. Pike has been there long enough to know everybody in the village. There are not often strangers about at that time. — I have the honour to be, sir, your obedient servant, — A. BUCHANAN, Superintendent.*"

Not one of Buchanan's points can be taken seriously:

- Crouch undoubtedly could not hear or see well from his vantage point.
- It would not be in the least unusual for Pike to go twice to Chisenbury during the course of an evening. Apart from two hostelries in Enford, the only other public house on Ernest's patch was the Red Lion at Chisenbury, and it was a part of his duty to see it closed. We see from his statement of duty that he visited The Swan twice.
- It was true that there were legal provisions in the Licensing Consolidation Act of 1910 which was often used for the

prosecution of publicans accused of 'harbouring' a policeman on duty, the offence being considered a particular threat to police discipline in rural areas. But for Buchanan to suggest that all three Phillimores were lying merely because of fear of such action is a transparent attempt to influence the Chief Constable's view of the matter. Walter was a respected businessman and member of the Enford Parish Council.

- Buchanan dismisses Ernest's claim he saw two men on the road, simply because the bobby did not know who they were, implying that this must therefore be a lie. Why should Ernest lie about this? He might just as easily have said that he saw nobody. Had they been vagrants they would avoid the attention of policemen whose duty it was to move them out of the parish, or they might have been men on their way back to the nearby airfield which had brought many strangers to the area.[43] Even if they had been local, they would have been muffled against the wind, and difficult to see in the dark. It might be asked why Pike did not try to find out who the two men were in order to support his *alibi*, but it must be remembered that the case was trivial at this point, only acquiring greater significance once Pike realised he was going to be charged. By then Pike no doubt thought the evidence he had was quite sufficient to defend himself successfully. Why should he go wasting time looking for two strangers?

On the evening of 5th March Crouch went to Chisenbury with the intention of inquiring into Pike's *alibi*. He asked William Jennings, landlord of the Red Lion, whether anybody had left his pub at 10.00 the previous night; if anybody had, even one person, it would disprove Ernest's account of watching the pub closely, for he had said that nobody had left at closing time.

Jennings story supported Ernest's account though. "*No*", he said in answer to Crouch's question, "*we never get anybody in here after 8.30*

---

[43] The Upavon Flying School drew personnel from the Royal Flying Corps and the Royal Naval Air Service, the first Commandant being Captain G M Paine R.N. who would soon occupy Littlecott House. The military establishment of the School in 1912/13 was for 112 permanent staff and 68 students in addition to civilian employees.

of an evening". Jennings locked the door three minutes before 10 p.m., and then on the hour he heard steps outside. Somebody tested the door, and finding it secure, walked quickly on. Who could this have been? Ernest Pike, about his normal duty perhaps? If it was, it is unfortunate that he forgot to mention it in his own report, but as the act of trying the door would have been a virtually automatic action by the constable it is easy to see why he might have overlooked reporting it. As Crouch's evidence was never fully disclosed to him he would not subsequently have become aware of the value of what Jennings had said. If it was not Pike who rattled the door at 10 p.m., it can only have been a stranger, and Pike had claimed to have seen an unidentified man near the Red Lion at 10 p.m. Jennings' evidence should have been very helpful to Pike as it confirmed things that he could only have known for certain if he was indeed outside the Red Lion at the time he claimed to be there.

Thursday 6th March 1913

Pike had still not formally been charged with any offence, but he must have been concerned, knowing that Buchanan had called Phillimore to Amesbury and Crouch had been on his patch making enquiries. On Thursday 6th, William Keating called on the Pikes in order to say farewell before they left the area for Colerne and Ernest told the vicar of the events of the Tuesday night.

"*There is something behind all this*", he said, and went on to remark that he thought that he might not get justice, and so he should resign and "*go for*" Crouch, disturbing words given hindsight, but obviously the vicar did not construe them as a threat of violence.

"*They can do what they like, though*", said Pike, according to Keating's later account, "*but they cannot separate us*".

"*I hope not*", said Keating, continuing with tragic irony, "*I hope that brighter days will come, and you will be happy where you are going*".

Saturday 8th March 1913

The Chief Constable had called for a further report from Crouch which was forwarded on this day, in which the Sergeant recounted his Chisenbury investigations of 5th March. It was forwarded to Llewellyn by Buchanan with a covering note from the superintendent which desperately, but inaccurately insisted "*If Pike was at Chisenbury, as he says he was, someone must have seen him*". Buchanan still did not make any reference to being told of any meeting between Phillimore and Pike at Chisenbury.

Monday 10th March 1913

The Enford Parish Council routinely met under its Chairman, the Reverend Walter Haigh Branfoot, vicar of Enford. Before the main business of the evening was tackled the following resolution was moved, "*That the Enford Parish Council desires to place on record its appreciation of the helpful and conscientious way in which P.C. Pike has discharged his duties during the time he has been stationed in the parish*". The resolution was carried unanimously and the parish clerk was instructed to send a copy of it to the Chief Constable.

In the evening Crouch visited Enford once more, and informed Pike that he was to be charged with being in the Three Horse Shoes on the night of 4th March. He showed the constable the official charge sheet, and by the light of the sergeant's bicycle lamp Ernest wrote his simple defence in pencil in the space provided on the blue document.

Tuesday 11th March 1913

The charge sheet was forwarded to Llewellyn from Amesbury. Ernest might as well not have bothered to defend himself, for if the animosity that Buchanan nurtured towards him is in any doubt, then surely this document and its covering letter will remove it from the mind of even the most sceptical reader.

NATURE OF CHARGE	DEFENCE
1st - Being in a public house whilst on duty. 2nd - Telling a lie to a superior officer when accused of charge No.1.	This charge is entirely false. I have committed no such offence. I respectfully ask for the Chief Constable's full investigation.

Superintendent's Opinion

Sir, - After the enquiries that Sergeant Crouch has made, I have no doubt whatsoever that Pike was in the public-house. His wife told Sergeant Crouch that he was in the village, and Pike cannot mention anyone who saw him at Chisenbury. **I also ask you to notice the disrespectful way he has answered the charge** (author's emphasis). Your obedient servant, A. BUCHANAN, Supt.

A further charge of lying has already been added, three weeks before the Chief Constable was to hear the case. Ernest Pike is already guilty because the Superintendent says he is. By the standards of any time or place, how could Buchanan possibly have thought Crouch's sparse evidence to be so conclusive, or Pike's written response to be disrespectful? His comments speak volumes about his attitude, and about the entire case against Pike.

Wednesday 12th March 1913

The formal charge having been made, Ernest was now in a position to submit his own report to which we have already referred, and here for the first time that we know of, the Chisenbury meeting between him and Phillimore is documented. The report supported by a statement from Tom Phillimore, was forwarded to Devizes the next day, but being covered by another of Buchanan's poisonous specialities, could have done him little good.

THE CAST ASSEMBLES

"Sir," writes Buchanan, *"I have the honour to forward this report from P.C. Pike respecting the duty he states he performed on Tuesday, the 4th inst. (March) also a statement which Pike obtained himself from the landlord's son, but no doubt written by Pike and signed afterwards."*

It was then and still is standard practise for a witness's statement to be handwritten by a police officer so long as it is signed by the deponent, but as Pike was personally involved in this case, then another officer should have been detailed to obtain it. However, nobody in the police was helping him, and Pike had been told to gather in any supporting statements himself.

Monday 17th March 1913

Buchanan forwarded six further witness statements to Llewellyn. These were from A. Raymond, James Dear, Charles Phillimore, John Spreadbury, Emma Phillimore and Amelia Pike. All but Amelia's were written in Pike's hand, but signed by the respective witnesses.

Friday 28th March 1913

All concerned were given notice that the case would be heard by the Chief Constable at Amesbury during the afternoon of Monday 31st March when Llewellyn, accompanied by Archibald Buchanan's elder brother Robert, would be making a regular round of inspection in the south of the county.

Sunday 30th March 1913

As if the malevolence of men were not enough, fate played the Pike family yet another bad card from her deck, for the Chairman of the Standing Joint Committee, the Earl of Pembroke, died unexpectedly of a seizure in the dining room of the Regina Hotel in Rome. He had held the appointment since the Marquis of Bath relinquished it in 1906 when elevated to his forty year chairmanship of the County Council. Bath retained a seat on the S.J.C. but Vice-Chairman Henry Medlicott J.P. now temporarily occupied the chair pending the appointment of yet another peer of the realm. Though it would be immensely convenient for Llewellyn, it is difficult to imagine a worse choice from the Pike point of view than Jacob Pleydell-Bouverie, 6th Earl Radnor, who would be confirmed as chairman a little over three weeks later.

Monday 31st March 1913

Although Salisbury City had its own borough force, there was also a Salisbury division of the County Constabulary which was responsible for the surrounding district and Llewellyn visited them during the course of the morning accompanied by Superintendent Robert Buchanan. It was afternoon when the two men arrived at the splendid new station at Amesbury. Five men were in the room where the hearing against the Enford bobby was held; Llewellyn, the two Buchanans, Crouch and Pike. The only record of exactly what was said comes of course from the three who were still alive the following morning and it is sure that at the very least they would have placed the best possible interpretation (from their point of view) on the events. Even so, from what they admitted of the procedure, it can be seen to have been a sham.

The Quality of Evidence

The disciplinary hearing, simple though it was, should have treated evidence in accordance with normal rules. The best sort of testimony is direct or primary evidence, that is when witnesses say from personal knowledge that they saw, heard, felt or did something. Circumstantial evidence, that which leads one to presume a fact from the existence of another, is still acceptable but does not carry such weight as primary evidence. It is not of course a simple matter of 'primary evidence always beats circumstantial', but strong corroborative factors usually need to be adduced to make a legally convincing case out of circumstantial testimony. By any standard the primary evidence in Pike's favour overwhelmed Crouch's laughably weak story which should have been laughed out of court, but that wasn't the way things worked in county constabularies in 1913.

Pike had cheered up since saying to William Keating on 6th March that he feared he would not get justice. He set out for Amesbury in good heart; he had an *alibi* in the correct sense of the word, "*I was elsewhere*", by virtue of Walter Phillimore's evidence of the Chisenbury meeting, two other witnesses who could give primary evidence, and five corroborative statements which testified to his earlier movements.

The charges were read out, as was the report of Frank Crouch, though Pike complained within the few hours of life now left to him that he did not know all that Crouch had put in against him. Pike said the charge was untrue, but when Crouch said he had been standing only ten yards away from the door of the Three Horse Shoes, Pike said,

"*You are wrong Sergeant, and you know you are wrong.*"

When Llewellyn came to Pike's *alibi*, he turned it against the constable with a cynical distortion of logic,

"*How did you know it was Phillimore that you saw?*"

"*I recognised him.*"

"*Well then, why did you not recognise the two men that you said you saw?*"

To that, Llewellyn later said, Pike had no answer. Of course he had no answer to such a twisted question and he must by now have simply given up trying. Whilst going to such bizarre lengths to throw doubt upon the *alibi* though, Llewellyn still made no objection to Pike's claim to have mentioned it to Crouch on the 4th March. The Chief was obviously influenced by Archibald Buchanan, because he now asked Pike why he had gone twice to Chisenbury, a point that Buchanan falsely claimed to be unusual.

The Chief Constable found Pike guilty on both charges made against him, and moved on to the punishment. By Llewellyn's later account it was, in the first instance, to have been a reprimand, despite all, a fairly minor award. But Llewellyn decided that he would increase this in view of what he called Pike's "*abusive language*" to Crouch. We have seen from Buchanan's letters what constituted 'disrespectful' language, so we can assume the words "*You are wrong and you know you are wrong*", when spoken by a constable to a sergeant constituted abuse and because of it, Pike was sentenced to forfeit his merit class grade.

Once again then he was to be posted to a new duty station under a cloud having been degraded, when only a short time earlier he might justifiably have been hoping to move on promotion. It must have been a bitter pill to swallow, but if only matters had been allowed to finish at this point then two men might have lived. But the man behind the desk was not quite done. In front of the two superintendents and Sergeant Crouch, he would now give a little 'friendly' advice to the humiliated constable.

"You should stop making friends of publicans. All your offences have been brought about through drink."

"And you have an 'outside friend' who is no good to you." Ernest must finally thought to himself that Llewellyn had at last got to the heart of why he was being persecuted. Without the name having been mentioned he blurted out:

"The Reverend Keating is nothing to me"

"Oh I am glad that you know who I am talking about", countered Llewellyn, going on to criticise the clergyman's visits which he had previously accepted to be acts of kindness. Who else but Archibald Buchanan can be to blame for this change of mind?

Exactly what was said next was later hotly disputed. In his last few hours of life Pike would allege that Llewellyn had said that there was village tittle tattle linking Amelia with Keating, but the Chief and the other survivors of the conversation always subsequently carefully denied this, their line being that Pike had somehow put a wild and uncalled for construction on innocent and well-meant advice from a benevolent Chief Constable. Pike rounded on Crouch and accused him of telling lies about him and his family, and at this point, thanks to Llewellyn's insensitivity, the two men's fate was sealed and they entered the final six hours of their lives.

The hearing was then ended. Meeting up with their respective colleagues, Pike and Crouch now mounted their bicycles and set off home, north along the Avon valley to meet their destinies.

Chapter 5

Realisation
The Bodies are Discovered
Coombe Tuesday 1st April 1913 – The Morning

When he answered the telephone at breakfast time on the Tuesday at his home at Etchilhampton House near Devizes, it must surely have passed through the Chief Constable's mind, however briefly, that this must all be a joke in very bad taste. After all, it *was* All Fools Day. But that reaction would not have lasted longer than a fraction of a second. Llewellyn's thoughts must have immediately turned to the bad tempered incident over which he had presided at Amesbury only 16 hours previously. If the corpse was that of Crouch then the Enford man must surely be a suspect!

Let us for now leave the Chief Constable at home with what we can well imagine his thoughts must have been about his own rôle in the matter, and go to Coombe where we shall pick up the train of events.

At six o'clock that morning four labourers had met at the crossroads prior to setting off for work at the Army Flying Sheds. As they stood chatting, one, chancing to look along the footpath which led across the northern extremity of the field known as Long Ground, saw a huddled shape some twenty yards from where they were standing. The daylight was good enough to see that it was a man, and the group ran to render what assistance they could. Reaching the spot they found an obviously lifeless form lying face down. Although the face was obscured, that it was Sergeant Frank Crouch they had no doubt, as the three silver stripes on the sleeve of the police uniform were visible, and the helmet lay close by. He was obviously dead, a fact testified to by the enormous wound to the left of his head, out of which brain tissue had been ejected onto the surrounding ground by some terrible force. Two fired twelve bore shotgun cartridges laying in the grass near the body mutely answered their unasked questions.

REALISATION, THE BODIES ARE DISCOVERED

They did not move the body, and made an attempt to alert the nearest policeman, not unnaturally thought to be Pike. Coombe Farm was connected to the telephone system with two separate lines, one for Mr Maton's own use and the other for his farm manager. Even though few police stations in the county were connected – certainly not a little cottage like Pike's house – the message could still have been relayed quickly through other subscribers, or even via the operator at Enford Post Office, just across the road from Ernest's cottage.

Even if nobody in Enford was answering telephones at that time of the morning, a fit and frightened man could run the distance in about 10 minutes if Mr Maton's motor car was not made available. But Pike was not at home said Amelia who had risen about half an hour before the first knock came at her door. She had not been particularly alarmed by her husband's overnight absence, as this often happened when there were fires on his patch, not a rare occurrence in an area where thatch was common. She must have become increasingly worried though as the minutes wore on and the rumours started to fly, especially when she noticed that her husband's shotgun was missing.

The news moved quickly. P.C. Slade of Upavon, Pike's cycling companion of the previous afternoon, was on the scene with Dr Augustus L. Edwards of Upavon by 6.30 a.m., only half an hour after the body was first discovered. Slade, who only twelve hours earlier had heard Pike say *"I will make this county ring!"* must have been the first to suspect the identity of the killer. In his subsequent inquest evidence, Slade would say that after seeing the body he made arrangements to inform the Chief Constable. Although this makes it sound as though he did this directly, neither the accepted protocol of rank, nor the timings can support such a direct approach, for Hoël Llewellyn's nightmare call was not received by him until 8.15. Slade would normally notify his immediate superior, but as that person lay shattered in Long Ground, he would have made contact with the inspector's station at Ludgershall or the divisional station at Amesbury. But even the smart new Amesbury station was not connected to the telephone system, through the parsimony of the

REALISATION, THE BODIES ARE DISCOVERED

Standing Joint Committee. The gap in electrical communications might explain why it took a further hour and a half for the message to finally reach Llewellyn even though he was himself connected to the telephone at his home.[45]

The news reached the Police H.Q. at Devizes at about 8.00 a.m. Superintendent Robert Buchanan quickly hired a car from Messrs Willis of Central Garage, Devizes in which he travelled to the Chief Constable's house at Etchilhampton, fortunately located on the way from Devizes towards Enford. Robert at this stage would have been able to appraise the Chief of Pike's disappearance, for his brother Archibald had also jumped to the obvious conclusion, and had visited the Enford station to check on Pike's whereabouts.

Llewellyn did not delay in setting off to Coombe, arriving there at 9.15 having briefly stopped at Pike's cottage on the way. He had declined to take the handsome hired vehicle, inviting Robert Buchanan to join him in Mr Maton's car which the farmer had thoughtfully sent to collect him. Willis's car was not wasted though, for Llewellyn consigned his bloodhound couple, Moonlight and Flair, together with their handler P.C. Wilson to it. We can imagine this unlikely convoy, wooden-spoked artillery wheels rattling over the flint roads, the Chief Constable leading the way and the two big, baying hounds, heads out of the windows, ears flying in the wind, noses sniffing the air, following close behind.[46]

---

[45] A meeting of the Wiltshire Standing Joint Committee at Trowbridge on 30th January 1913 had bickered about the cost of installing the new-fangled device in the Police Station. The Chief Constable had commented to the meeting on the necessity of connecting stations including Amesbury, Netheravon and Upavon, but Earl Radnor resisted it because of the cost of £5 per installation. When Sir John Goldney pointed out to the meeting that '*The Policeman should be the centre of communications in the villages*' and thus needed a telephone, Radnor's inspired response was "*Might I suggest then that he borrows someone else's?*" Approval for the installation of a *second* telephone in the Chief Constable's home at Etchilhampton had however been given at an S.J.C. meeting on 30th November 1912. Netheravon Station was eventually connected on 14th November 1913. The holy of holies of the English Police Service, Scotland Yard, was first connected to the telephone system in 1901.

[46] Llewellyn was convinced of the effectiveness of dogs in police work. Shortly after taking command of Wiltshire Force, he had been impressed by Wilson's blood hound 'Shadower'. He bought two of his pups, and persuaded the Standing Joint Committee to meet the costs of their upkeep, Moonlight and Flair thus becoming the first permanent

Calling at Pike's cottage on the way to Coombe, Llewellyn confirmed what he must already have suspected, that Pike had not been home all night. By this time, about 9.00 a.m., Amelia must have been very agitated, as news of the discovery of Crouch's body would have spread throughout the valley and the visits of Buchanan and Llewellyn clearly indicated that suspicion was fixed on her husband.

A couple of miles to the south, in Netheravon, Mrs Alice Kate Crouch was similarly distraught, having been gently warned that her husband had met with an accident, and that she should prepare herself for the worst. One report tells us that she immediately ran to a neighbour's house, and collapsed just inside the door exclaiming "*I'm sure my husband is dead, and Pike has killed him*". Eighty-six years later, Ivy Punter, then an 11 year old schoolgirl in Netheravon, told the author that she remembered being told by her teacher that "*Wilfred* (Crouch's eldest son) *will not be at school today*". He never did return for the Crouch family were moved very quickly from Netheravon, first to a police house in Mrs Crouch's home town of Devizes and later to a private residence.

Llewellyn did not tarry at Enford, staying only long enough to satisfy himself that Pike had not returned home the night before, that his gun was missing, and to obtain a waistcoat belonging to Ernest, which he would use to give scent to the sensitive noses of Moonlight and Flair. Arriving at Coombe at 9.15 a.m. Llewellyn, dressed that morning in Norfolk jacket and plus fours, took control over the investigation,

---

officially funded operational police dogs in England. Wilson was transferred from his station in Ogbourne St George near Marlborough to Police Headquarters in Devizes to care for the four legged sleuths. Llewellyn got good results from his hounds, and he wrote to '*The Field*' in February 1912 extolling the virtues of the breed. In January 1913 he dispatched Wilson together with one and a half couple, Moonlight, Flair and Shadower, on loan to the chief Constable of West Sussex, where they were spectacularly effective in assisting in the capture of two rick burners named Wakeford and Chant who received long prison sentences (7 and 5 years). As a bonus they also caught two chicken thieves (human) who were less drastically dealt with. Llewellyn urged his men to acquire dogs to accompany them on their beats, recommending Irish Terriers, or Airedales and persuaded the county authorities to provide funds to recompense policemen for the cost of dog licences, once the animals had been approved by him. He was fond of dogs and exhorted his men in touching terms to take good care of their canine pals. On 14th May 1913, when the controversy surrounding the two policemen's deaths was at its height, he held the first show for policemen's dogs at Devizes.

Plate h: The Crouch family

seeing to the removal of the body on a cart to farm buildings near Mr Maton's house. Police suspicion was naturally very firmly fixed on Ernest Pike, but at this stage they assumed that they were embarking on a search for an armed fugitive, so firearms were issued to a number of officers whilst the following description was circulated throughout Wiltshire and the constabularies of neighbouring counties:

Age 39. Height five feet 11 inches. Complexion fair. Eyes, grey. Hair and moustache, brown. Slim build. May be armed. May be on bicycle.

These were sensible steps to take, but were rendered superfluous within 90 minutes thanks to the efforts of Moonlight and Flair. Being laid on at the spot where Crouch's body was found, the two useful beasts quickly led off across a short stretch of grass to the narrow track leading from the Coombe cross roads towards the river. Nowadays a footpath, this track was at the time sufficiently wide to take carts, and the river crossing to Fifield consisted of a footbridge for pedestrians and a ford for hooves and wheels.

Here, some 150 yards from the place where Crouch lay, hounds lost scent but it didn't matter for in the shallows below the bridge, two or three yards from the bank and not even totally immersed in water lay Pike's shotgun. We may safely guess that this discovery was made somewhere between 9.30 and 9.45 a.m. On being retrieved from the water, it was noticed that the hammer positions indicated a fired cartridge in the right barrel and a live one in the left. Llewellyn safely fired off the cocked barrel.

A picture of events was now starting to emerge. The gun in the water was almost certainly the one to have been used by Crouch's killer. Llewellyn knew from the two ejected cartridges by the body that the double-barrelled gun had probably been reloaded immediately after the fatal shots had been fired. The discovery of this gun with a fired round in only one barrel indicated that the gun had not simply been discarded by a fleeing killer intent on preserving his own life, but that it had been fired again, and this time a single round had been sufficient to meet the shooter's purpose. That Pike had shot Crouch had been a good bet ever since P.C. Slade had first heard the news of the finding of the sergeant's body three hours earlier, but now it was beginning to look like the search for Ernest Pike would result in the discovery of another corpse.

A decision was taken to drag the river, and hooked poles were quickly fabricated. March 1913 had been a very wet month in south Wiltshire, thundery rain falling nearly every day, and so the water was flowing high and fast. A small number of policemen from the surrounding area were on the scene aided by locals who had been attracted by the unfolding drama, and all were put to work under the close supervision of dog handler Wilson.

The crowd split in two, steadily working downstream on both banks, with Wilson on the left (eastern) bank. At about 11 o'clock, a quarter of a mile downstream from the Fifield footbridge, a cry went up from the right bank; something had been found trapped by weed. Harry Harding, the groom who had seen Frank Crouch by the Netheravon Post Office the previous evening, could see the spot across the water

Plate i: Chief Constable and Coroner at the White Bridge

meadows from the stables at Haxton Farm where he worked for Farmer Notley.

He joined Wilson and together they crossed the river just in time to see Ernest Pike's body being hauled onto the bank. An unhinged door was brought to do service as a stretcher, and the corpse was carried to a shed in Fifield. It was not badly mutilated, having been in sweet flowing water for only twelve hours which had washed away the blood from light external wounding around the right ear. Those who cared to look more closely might have noticed other wounds inside the mouth. Nobody present could now doubt the sequence of the previous night's events and Llewellyn gave instructions for the police alert to be stood down. Shortly afterwards the Reverend Walter Branfoot accompanied by a police constable, knocked at the door of the Enford cottage to break the appalling news to Amelia.

REALISATION, THE BODIES ARE DISCOVERED

The reason why Pike chose his spot to die is easy to understand. An experienced policeman with nearly twenty years' service and a countryman to boot, he is certain to have had knowledge of gunshot wounds. He would know that survival, though with hideous mutilation, occurs in a surprising number of suicide attempts – often a weapon is fired slightly prematurely as it is being awkwardly manoeuvred into position for the anticipated fatal blast. From the moment that he shot his sergeant he was a dead man, but being determined to perish by his own hand rather than on the gallows, he would have stood in the river in order to die by drowning in case his shooting attempt were to result only in unconsciousness.

Some subsequent accounts suggest that Pike sat on the handrail of the bridge, and fell backwards into the water. There is no evidence to support this. Had it happened in this way it is likely that the effects of recoil would have caused the gun to fall on the bridge rather than in the water where it was found.

Chapter 6

Inquisition Super Visum Corporis
Coombe, Tuesday 1st April 1913 – Afternoon

If this story were fiction, it would stretch credibility too far to introduce yet another official whose behaviour lays him open to criticism, but reality now compels us to meet Frederick Arthur Percy Sylvester. A solicitor and commissioner for oaths with a practise in Trowbridge, he was Registrar and High Bailiff of Trowbridge County Court and also His Majesty's Coroner for mid-Wiltshire and therefore had responsibility for the inquest into the fatalities at Coombe. Before we look at the way he discharged it though, it is necessary to consider some duties of a coroner's court in 1913, which differed in a number of very significant ways from current practice.

Plate j: Temporary Mortuary. Llewellyn leaves the shed in Fifield where Pike's body lay.

Coroners Courts and Verdicts

From being Keepers of the Pleas of the Crown, the historically wide ranging duties of coroners gradually contracted over the centuries as other courts developed, until a few years before the end of the nineteenth century when they were eventually restricted to inquiries into unnatural deaths and treasure trove.[47]

---
[47] Coroner's Act 1887

INQUISITION SUPER VISUM CORPORIS

Although the responsibility for appointing coroners was given to the new County Councils by the Local Government Act of 1888, jurisdiction over inquests continued, very properly, to be retained by the judiciary.

For centuries, inquests took place with coroner and jury sitting around the dead body. Although this potentially pungent practise has long since been consigned to the past, a relic of it still existed in 1913, for it was still compulsory for the proceedings to be held '*super visum corporis*', that is after the viewing of the body by both the coroner and the jury.[48] Certain legal and pathological functions such as post mortem examinations could not be authorised until the inquest had been formally opened and the viewing carried out, and difficulties in retarding decomposition - especially as inquests were still usually held near to the scene of the death, where proper mortuary facilities would often be unavailable - meant that it was necessary for coroners to act with much more celerity than nowadays.

But there was also another reason for speed. Inquests still played a significant part in the investigation of crime, and though by the beginning of the twentieth century the police were the obvious authority to take the principal rôle in investigating and prosecuting homicide, a 1910 Home Office Committee had encouraged the ancient use of inquests as a means of obtaining information about fatal crimes. From 1926 until 1977 any potential criminal proceedings were notified to the coroner by the police so that automatic adjournments would be granted once the simple medical and identification evidence had been given, thus preventing the opinion of a coroner's jury prejudicing the fair trial of the person alleged to have responsibility for the death.

Since 1977 a coroner's court must make no allusion at any time whatever to the identity of any person who might be considered responsible for causing the death of another, and must be scrupulous in avoiding any intimation of blame or liability for any offence.[49] But

[48] This requirement was finally abolished by the 1926 Coroner's (Amendment) Act.
[49] A requirement confirmed by the Master of the Rolls. See, R v Coroner for N. Humberside and Scunthorpe – Times Law Report of 28th April 1994 'No function

the 1887 Act, still in full unamended force in 1913 had made it a specific duty of coroners' juries to state the name of the person they believed to be guilty of causing the death in any case of homicide, be it murder or manslaughter. Any murder verdict naming a killer which might be made by a coroner's jury was only accusatory though. His or her identification by name in the Bill of Inquisition (the coroner's document setting out the inquest verdict) did not convict, but had the same effect as a Grand Jury finding 'True Bill' on a Bill of Indictment, that is to say that it was the authority to commit the accused person for trial at a court of Assize.

Insanity had long been a common defence to a murder charge and the law accepted 'Guilty but Insane' as a verdict which would incarcerate the killer at the Sovereign's Pleasure, but at least spare him from the gallows. In the period 1908-1913, 34.2% of all murderers were found to be legally insane or unfit to plead, a proportion which increased to a little under one half by the eve of the Second World War as juries became increasingly inclined to accept the defence where they felt that a death penalty was not appropriate.

At the end of 1911 the country's secure asylums held 1119 individuals described as 'criminal lunatics', of whom 470 had been indicted for murder. In 1913 a legal responsibility was placed upon the police to report any evidence of mental imbalance to a court before which such a person might be arraigned.[50]

Insanity pleas only significantly declined from 1957 when the law began to recognise 'non-capital' categories of murder, and the concept of 'diminished responsibility' became a legally acceptable method of translating a homicide charge from murder into manslaughter, lawyers recommending their homicidal clients to forgo insanity pleas on the reasoning that if they were to be incarcerated, then prison would be preferable to the asylum.

The 1913 coroner's jury though, as distinct from the petty jury in a murder trial, was not allowed to consider insanity in murder cases,

---

of inquest to attribute blame or responsibility'.
[50] Mental Deficiency Act 1913 s 2

even if it was as clear as day to them that the killer was as mad as a hatter. They simply had to find a murder verdict in homicide cases, if that was what the evidence led them to believe, and name the killer, if they could. Any amelioration by virtue of a defence of insanity then had to be introduced at the subsequent murder trial. By and large this worked well, where the killer was still alive. However, cases of murder followed by the suicide of the assailant caused an anomaly, as the accused person would never have the opportunity to offer any defence in court. The law, as it stood, could do nothing about this, and the stigma of an accusation of murder remained against the dead killer's name, even if it was obvious that, had he lived, an insanity plea would have been entered as a defence.

The suicide verdict was a different matter. Since 1961 it has been no crime to take one's own life, and police intervention to stop an individual committing an act which is not unlawful is predicated on their interpretation of their powers under section 136 of the 1983 Mental Health Act. The familiar construction 'whilst the balance of the mind was disturbed' used by coroners is now only a legally meaningless form of solace to the bereaved. But before 1961 suicide was a felony if committed by a person adjudged to be sane. The verdict on such a person would be *'felo de se'*, a 'felony upon himself', but a decision by a jury that it was committed whilst insane would reduce such a verdict and its post mortem penalties. The sane act was regarded with particular horror in earlier times. Sir John Jervis, writing in 1829 in the first edition of his standard work on coronership, elegantly and passionately expressed the common view thus:

"Self-murder is wisely and religiously considered by English Law as the most heinous description of felonious homicide; for, as no man hath power to destroy life but by commission of God, the author of it, the Suicide is guilty of a double offence; one spiritual, invading the prerogative of the Almighty, and rushing into His presence uncalled for; and the other temporal, against the King, who has an interest in the preservation of all his subjects. This offence, therefore, is ranked by law amongst the highest crimes, making it a peculiar species of felony, a felony upon oneself."

Until only six years before Jervis wrote this, suicides were still buried at crossroads, the bodies transfixed by a stake. From 1823 churchyard burial was permitted, but the interment had to be at night and without Christian rites, a situation which continued throughout much of the century until in 1882 a more normal burial was finally permitted. But even then the local bishop's permission had to be obtained, and the Church of England burial service could not be used. Until 1870 the suicide's estate had been subject to escheat, the forfeiture of assets to the Crown, so with the exception of any difficulties which might be encountered by the soul of a departed self-felon at the Pearly Gates, the harshness of the law was suffered on earth by the family, not only in financial terms, but also in the price of shame.

Now, English juries have always tended to soften the effects of harsh law, and at suicide inquests they usually needed very little encouragement to find verdicts allowing that the deceased had acted under the pressures of insanity. Such verdicts were the norm.[51] Chief Constable J.T. Coleman of Lincoln in 1908 obviously found such compassion distasteful. He complained that of the 3434 suicide inquests reported in England in 1907, the vast majority resulted in verdicts of 'temporary insanity'. Coleman knew better, identifying the real causes as "fast living, gambling, greed and ungodliness".

The Coroner's Court at Coombe – Preparations

It was still the usual practice in 1913 for inquest proceedings to take place close to the place where bodies had been discovered, and in rural areas this was nearly always done in the same village. Almost any building would suffice for a court room, only licensed premises normally being excluded, though even they might still be used *in extremis*. The inquests into the deaths of William Frank Crouch and Ernest Pike were therefore held at Coombe, and the obvious place to serve the purpose was the large farmhouse belonging to Mr Maton.

---

[51] See 'Dictionary of English Law' by W J Byrne, Sweet and Maxwell, London 1923 for confirmation that temporary insanity verdicts were overwhelmingly the norm in suicide cases.

Criticism about the timing of inquests after death was not at all unknown, but was always concerned with delay, so much so that a late nineteenth century High Court decision had actually found it necessary to lay down that a coroner who did not perform an inquest within four days of the death being reported to him was in dereliction of his duty. Contrarily though, subsequent criticism of the Coombe inquest was that it was too quick, not permitting a full revelation of facts. But how quick is 'quick'? Before answering that, we will look at what had to happen to get the inquest opened.

The first step was for Mr Sylvester to be notified of the deaths. Though instructions to the Wiltshire police promulgated two years later made it clear that any constable should be prepared to make immediate and direct contact with the coroner without necessarily going through any police chain of command[52] they were under no such orders in 1913, and P.C. Slade, the first policeman on the scene after the deaths, communicated via his superiors.

We know from later statements that the notification to Mr Sylvester of Frank Crouch's death was made by telephone by Captain Llewellyn himself (both he and the Coroner were telephone subscribers at home and at their offices), and we can guess that it was one of the first things which he did after hearing the news at 8.15 a.m. on the Tuesday morning. After a decision as to the time of the inquest had been made, Mr Blunt, the Coroner's officer, then had to travel to the site to make the necessary arrangements, assisted by the local police, to find suitable premises and empanel a jury after Mr Sylvester had signed an authorising warrant.

The earliest train that Blunt could have caught would have been the 9.33 a.m. which reached Devizes at 10.00. Assuming that motor transport met him there, he would then have arrived at Coombe by about 11 a.m., by which time the situation had changed dramatically. As Blunt left Trowbridge, neither Pike's body nor gun had been discovered, and so there was no intimation of suicide, but as Blunt arrived at Coombe, Pike's body was being pulled from the river. It

---
[52] Force General Order No 162 of 16th November 1915.

must surely have been at this point that a decision was taken to hold both inquests concurrently. Blunt then had to select the specified number of jurors from the electoral roll and summon them. Witnesses had to be informed, exhibits gathered. The Coroner then had to be advised that all was in order and travel from Trowbridge to Coombe. All was arranged, and a time was set for the opening of the inquests. It was to be 3.30 p.m. on Tuesday 1st April 1913, just 270 minutes after the discovery of Ernest Pike's body. Quick, by any standard.

The outline of the previous night's events must surely have seemed obvious to everybody, and it is asking too much of human nature that both Sylvester and the jury should have brought completely open minds to the proceedings. Though circumstantial, the available evidence was quite compelling, but a very recent (1912) ruling by no less a judge than the Master of the Rolls (*Southall v Cheshire County News*) about the need to prove suicide and never to presume it, should have been firmly in the Coroner's mind. Suicide notes, always considered good evidence of intent, often take a few hours to come to light too. But even if such speed in commencing proceedings was desirable for hygienic reasons, the Coroner had the option of adjourning once the bodies had been viewed and medical evidence taken. Had he done so, further evidence would definitely have been before him and he must have known this to be very likely. But as we shall see, certain parties had good reason to fear the embarrassment from the evidence which would emerge if even a short adjournment or delay in the start of the inquest were allowed. What Sylvester must have known though was that Amelia Pike would be unable to obtain representation and would have to appear in a court which was undoubtedly going to accuse her husband of murder only four hours after she was informed of his violent death. In the event, Inspector Mark Elkins of Ludgershall called on her at ten minutes to three o'clock to give her just forty minutes notice that she was required to attend. There can be no doubt that there was an overriding desire in some quarters to get this inquest quickly wrapped up and finished with.

Coombe: Proceedings and Witnesses

The fifteen jurymen and witnesses had been summoned by Mr Blunt for 3.15 p.m. and most had arrived somewhat early, taking shelter from light rain under the dripping eaves of the farm buildings. Sylvester travelled by one of the frequent trains from Trowbridge to Devizes and then onwards to Coombe by courtesy of Willis's cars, but the impossible haste with which the whole business was arranged is indicated by his own delayed arrival, as he was some ten or so minutes late.

The Coroner opened the proceedings in court by asking a juror named Fred Pike if he was any relation to Ernest, and Fred, an old soldier, said no, he wasn't. Sylvester now showed that he had been well briefed, telling the court that they would hear of the relationship between the two dead men over the last few days.

"*From what we know of the case,*" he said (before any evidence had been heard), *I hope that you will be able to come to a verdict today and that it will not be necessary to adjourn."* In itself this was not an unreasonable thing to say, but in the whole context of the rush to bring things to a conclusion it acquires significance. Coroner's juries of the time tended to do much as they were told, and certainly the farm workers and labourers who made up the bulk of this one would know that they were expected to conclude the proceedings without delay. Without further ado Sylvester, the jury and certain witnesses visited the two temporary mortuaries, a process described in reports as 'taking some time'. As photographs show, Sylvester and Llewellyn were in close company at this stage. It would have taken the twenty or so men about twenty minutes when one considers that they would have to file past the bodies in the confined space of separate outlying sheds and farm buildings before returning to the farm office overlooking the semi-circular lawn at the front of Mr Maton's house.

The office-cum-courtroom was packed solid, and many men, including some of the jurors, were forced to stand, not because of a lack of chairs but simply because of insufficient space. In addition to the Coroner, Blunt his clerk, and the fifteen jurymen, there were other policemen including the Buchanan brothers and Inspector Elkins. There were witnesses, including Llewellyn who had taken a seat to the right of the Coroner, and ten newspapermen.

A photographer representing a London daily tried to enter the court with his camera but was ejected by police,[53] and he was reduced to snapping outside views. There must have been about forty people in the 20ft x 20ft room, with space further restricted by furniture and fitments. It didn't matter too much though – none of those present were to spend too long in there.

In came the witnesses, the very first of whom, James Cannings, made an unchallenged error. The airfield labourer gave evidence of the finding of Crouch's body. He said that it was lying close to the footpath *"in the field"* – he does not seem to have been a local man because it was necessary for a juror to interject the name of the field, Long Ground. The Coroner asked Cannings if this was in the hamlet of Coombe in the parish of Enford, to which Cannings mistakenly replied in the affirmative.[54] This was not of any great importance and did not affect the Coroner's area of jurisdiction but it indicates how haste led to imprecision. Cannings went on to tell how the sergeant had one hand in his pocket and the other was tucked into his tunic front, as if for warmth.

Next came P.C. William Slade of Upavon, who described how he was alerted and travelled to the scene with Doctor Augustus Edwards. When they arrived they found Crouch's body, which had not been moved, lying face down with the helmet close by. From a piece of wrapping paper in his pocket Slade now produced the fired shotgun cartridges which he had picked up that morning, and told how he alerted Superintendent Archibald Buchanan and the Chief Constable.

---

[53] At this time there was still no outright ban on the taking of photographs in an English court. It was up to the bench to permit it if they wished, so one must assume that the ejection at Coombe was the decision of Sylvester.

[54] All of Long Ground is in the parish of Fittleton, and the southern edge of the track to Fifield forms the boundary with Enford parish, of which Coombe is part. The sergeant's body definitely lay a few yards inside the parish of Fittleton until it was removed to Maton's buildings, on the Enford side of the parish boundary.

He was not present, he explained to the court, when Pike's body was found.

The flow of evidence progressed to the finding of the constable's corpse, and Harry Harding, the Haxton Farm groom, described his part. For some reason Sylvester asked this witness when he had last seen Sergeant Crouch, and it was now that the previous evening's meeting between the two men outside Netheravon Post Office at 7.45 p.m. was recorded. Although it wasn't mentioned in the court, Harding's parents lived in a small cottage which stands in the same terrace as the old Netheravon Post Office, where there was an outside two-faced clock, which comfortably explains why Harding was in the vicinity and why he was certain of the time.

After the warm up men had played their part, the stage was set for the major players to take their bow, and Captain Llewellyn took centre stage. He was asked by Sylvester to relate the tale of the hearing at Amesbury the previous day, and having given his brief version of it he was prompted to refer to Pike's previous disciplinary misdemeanours. This sort of evidence would have been inadmissible in most courts of the time as being likely to prejudice a jury[55], but a coroner's court is allowed great latitude in what it can hear and consider. Llewellyn went out of his way to say that Crouch's evidence had been *"exceptionally fair"* and that Superintendent Archibald Buchanan had *"spoken strongly in Pike's favour"*. Buchanan's written communications to Llewellyn on the subject of Pike had not yet entered the public domain. Llewellyn at that time could have had no idea that they eventually would, and probably thought that it would do him and Buchanan no good if he mentioned them. But knowing as we do what vitriol the Superintendent poured into his letters, it beggars belief that Llewellyn could have been telling the truth to the inquest about Buchanan's attitude towards the dead constable.

When the jury foreman, a Mr Tilley of Bottlesford (the village where Ernest had some years before first met the Reverend William Keating) asked the Chief if there had been any reason for him to suppose that

---

[55] This ancient Common Law protection was abolished by Criminal Justice Act of 2003.

Pike might do something desperate, the answer was, of course, negative.

The Coroner now took the opportunity to move on to some evidence of intent, and he recalled William Slade. The Upavon constable repeated Ernest's headline grabbing comment, "*I will make the county ring!*" and described his colleague as being upset, but said that he did not make any actual threat against anybody, and did not mention Crouch by name.

All eyes now turned to Amelia Pike, the small woman already attired in widows black and attended by a female companion. Her composure was described as remarkable, and indeed her capacity to be able to answer any questions in such circumstances and surroundings can only be described as heroic. Mr Sylvester is reported as treating her with great consideration, as indeed he should. The only time that she faltered was when Ernest's name was mentioned. Sylvester asked her whether Ernest had returned home at any time after leaving the house at 9 p.m.

"*No.*"

"*What sort of condition was he in when he returned from Amesbury?*"

"*Sad and distressed — broken hearted. He sat alone in the front room for a part of the time.*"

The answer to the next question must have been awaited with great interest, for even those present who had no previous inkling of Pike's disciplinary record were now aware of it by courtesy of the evidence given by Llewellyn at Sylvester's prompting.

"*Did he have anything to drink during the evening?*"

"*Only a part of a pint of ale with his supper sir.*"

The Coroner then indicated the shotgun which had been lying on a table since it had been produced during Llewellyn's evidence. Amelia was unable to say with certainty whether the weapon was that belonging to her husband, but confirmed that she had noticed that Ernest's gun was missing from home when she had risen that morning.

She was not able to say anything particularly helpful about the cartridge cases which had been produced by Slade, for all she knew was the colour of those usually used by her husband. With that she passed from the stage.

Fortunately Kate Crouch was not put through a similar ordeal. She did not attend the inquest.

The Wounds

Augustus Edwards, General Practitioner of Upavon described the condition of both bodies, and expressed his opinion on how the injuries causing death had occurred. Both men had obviously died from gunshot wounds to the head, that to Crouch appearing externally to be most severe. He had taken both barrels and the left side of his head and his brain had been removed by the shot.

This sort of explosive cranial injury, when inflicted by a shotgun is entirely characteristic of a contact shot, where the muzzles of the gun are in contact with the skin at the point of firing. The large quantity of gas generated by the deflagration of the propellant powder enters the cranium and creates huge internal pressures which can only be relieved by enormous rupturing of the head. The pellets from the shot – possibly two hundred in a 12 bore cartridge – will already have minced the brain tissue which will be ejected under the forces generated. Enough of the front of Frank Crouch's head remained for Dr Edwards to see that there was scorching of about 1½ inches diameter under the right of the chin, and a single entry wound near the left nostril.

From this description – and knowing that two spent cartridge cases had been recovered from beside the body – the clear indication is that both barrels were fired in rapid succession. The first blast may have missed, causing no more than scorching under the chin. The muzzles then seem to have been pushed closer into Crouch's face as the second barrel was fired. The fact that Crouch's hands remained inside his pocket and tunic front would indicate that he was taken by surprise, and that both shots were taken in very rapid succession. Edwards explained, with actions, how it could be that shots fired from the right might cause an entry wound on the left side of the face, stating his opinion, of which he was quite sure, that the wounds could not have been self-inflicted.

Ernest Pike's wounds, on the other hand he thought, were injuries made by a shot through the mouth fracturing the entire base of the skull, with some exit wounds over the right ear. Such intra-oral wounds are quite common in cases of suicide by firearm and no-one questioned the doctor's opinion. Gas pressure is often relieved by the corners of the mouth splitting, but Edwards did not mention this. He said that the cause of death had been the gunshot wound, not drowning.

The Summing Up

That concluded the evidence, and the Coroner now set about the important task of summing it up for the jury. He drew their attention to the fact that, clear though events seemed to be, the evidence relating to the sergeant's death was in fact circumstantial, and he then went on to remind them about Pike's bad disciplinary record. He took care to repeat the Chief Constable's assertions that Crouch and Buchanan had been generous in the way they both gave evidence at the Amesbury hearing the previous day, blaming only Pike for taking it badly. He made his own views about Crouch's demise clear, using the unfamiliar first Christian name:

"If you think — as I believe you will think — that the facts are so convincing as to leave no other option, then you must return a verdict of wilful murder against Ernest Pike. If you think there is a doubt you may say that William Crouch was found dead from gunshot wounds but as there was no evidence to say how they occurred then it is open to you to return an open verdict."

About the other death:

"Pike was very upset, and the doctor's evidence is very strong indeed that his wound was self-inflicted. If you think Pike committed the terrible and horrible crime, as to which at any rate there must be a strong suspicion in your minds,

it is your duty to return a verdict that he took his own life, otherwise called *felo de se*. If there is any doubt then you must return an open verdict."

Had proceedings started only a day later then any possible doubt would have been removed, for Ernest Pike had spent much of the three hours between arriving home from Amesbury and commencing his last patrol in writing three explicit suicide notes. Rather than leaving them to be found, he posted them and so at the time of the inquest they were in the mail. Besides making it crystal clear what he intended to do not only to himself but to Crouch as well, the notes would have thrown some light on Ernest's mental state, a factor that the jury expected to be required to deliberate upon.

"*Are we to consider the state of Pike's mind?*" asked Mr Tilley, the foreman speaking on behalf of the jurymen and presumably puzzled by Sylvester's omission of the common option. The Coroner's reply would surely have been instantly challenged had Amelia been represented by a lawyer:

"*Not in such a case as this.*"

The jury retired to another room to deliberate their findings. The verdict on Crouch must be murder, for an open verdict was not one which reasonable men would reach. But the range of their options in Pike's case, had been limited by the Coroner beyond what they had expected, as shown by Foreman Tilley's question. As an open verdict on Ernest Pike's death would have been as perverse as it would have been in Crouch's and as the Coroner had ruled out an insanity verdict, there was no real choice open to them. After a retirement of 15 minutes they returned to the court room to give their unanimous verdicts: William Frank Crouch had been wilfully murdered by Ernest Pike; Ernest Pike had committed *felo de se*. The foreman expressed the respectful feelings of the community towards both dead men and the entire jury donated their fees to the widows.[56]

---

[56] It was then common for certain individuals to be regularly called as inquest jurors. Such men would be assumed to be reliable, and to have a fair knowledge of procedures. It is not known whether Tilley was such a regular, but it might explain why he, a man from Bottlesford, some miles distant, was appointed foreman. If he *was* an experienced inquest juror, this would add much more significance to his question about consideration of sanity.

For the jury to record their respect towards a man whom the law compelled them to say had committed murder, and a crime held to be even worse than murder, was silently expressive of the feelings of truly unbiased people.

One last unresolved point remained. What date, asked the Coroner, should be entered on the death certificates? Dr Edwards had not been asked to opine on the times of death, but Mr Tilley replied that his jury were of the opinion that Ernest's suicide had occurred almost immediately after Frank Crouch's death, and so both men had officially breathed their last on March 31st 1913.[57]

The entire proceedings, from the Coroner's late arrival, and including the visit to both mortuary sites, the taking of evidence from six witnesses, and the fifteen minute jury retirement, had taken a little over an hour in total. As the members of the court and spectators left the farm house they may have seen a car carrying two anxious looking men arrive who asked where the inquest was taking place. Who they were would soon become apparent.

The Matons' servants started to rearrange the temporary court room, and as the gloomy assemblage dispersed, P.C. Keys may have been seen a few yards away performing a last service for his friend at the spot where he had fallen dead. He was burying the sergeant's brains.

Coming or Going?

Little attention was paid at the inquest to the question of whether Crouch had been killed whilst approaching or after leaving the meeting point. To consider the matter here is not wholly superfluous; it is interesting in its own right and it might also suggest whether Pike's mental state was one of uncontrollable rage or cold, calculating vengefulness.

---

[57] There is a report in one newspaper of a claim by a local resident to have seen a man with a gun wandering about the area of the footbridge very early the following morning. No such evidence was presented to the inquest, and there was never any further mention of this claimed sighting.

The orientation of Crouch's body, if we knew it, would give some indication, for as he fell face down then his head would probably have been pointing in the direction he was walking. This would be by no means conclusive – he might have turned around if he had heard a noise, but as his posture seemed to be completely relaxed when he was found the following morning, hands still in pockets, he does not seem to have been alarmed in the instant prior to death. The idea of him being thrown around by the gun blast may be discounted, for such things don't happen in reality – the energy in a bullet or shotgun load causes it to penetrate the body, not move it significantly. A man may stagger slightly in the last milliseconds of life even in the case of a very bad injury, but the collapsing motion of a person killed instantly by such enormous wounding to the head as that inflicted on Crouch is like that of a marionette where all strings have been simultaneously cut. The relative position of the scorching and entry wound suggests that Crouch had just started to turn to face his attacker.

One newspaper reporter out of all those present did opine that the meeting had taken place and that Pike then recovered his hidden gun and chased after Crouch. There is no evidential support for this idea, though as it was written by someone who was present at the inquest and would have questioned locals who had not been called as witnesses, it must be taken seriously. An examination of the mens' pocket notebooks might have helped, for they would have made entries had they met and Crouch would have signed Pike's entry. However, there is no record of such obvious evidence being considered in the obvious rush to conclude the inquest.

Perhaps the most significant indication as to what really happened lies in yet more evidence the inquest never had the chance to consider. That is the words that he wrote in his sitting room before setting off to Coombe. He made his intentions absolutely clear, and it is difficult to believe that with such dreadful purpose in his heart he could possibly have gone through the charade of a meeting with a man he intended to kill just seconds later. So, if Crouch was shot from the right as he approached the cross roads, then Pike had probably been hiding behind the earth bank at the side of Bamber Hill, the sunken lane which approached the cross roads from the south. Alternately, he may have taken cover amongst a row of elm trees which lined the path at the time. Pike's first shot may have missed despite being fired from a range of about a foot – all the indications are that he approached Crouch at speed, from the right, and fired before the sergeant realised anything was afoot.

Chapter 7

Correspondence, Funerals, Decisions, Resolutions

Apart from the macabre fragments disposed of by Keys, the rest of the sergeant's remains were buried with full honours at the parish church in his home village of Rowde at two o'clock the following Friday afternoon. It was a remarkable demonstration with over half of the entire County Constabulary present as well as police representatives from the Bath and Salisbury City forces.

Floral and written tributes had been received from colleagues and members of the public throughout Wiltshire and far beyond. A funeral parade headed by the Band of the 3rd Battalion of The Wiltshire Regiment (on whose badge the Constabulary had based theirs) formed up in Cock Road and joined with the family and coffin near the house of Frank Crouch's parents to make their way some 200 yards to the church. Robert Sterne, the retired Chief Constable, avoided the parade and proceeded straight to the church. Llewellyn was on horseback in full ceremonial rig including cocked hat, attended by his orderly P.C. Gearing. He had a full funereal programme on his hands each side of the weekend, for the following Monday he would be at Wilton for the service to despatch the soul of the Earl of Pembroke, late chairman of the Wiltshire Standing Joint Committee, whose noble remains had been brought from the Roman restaurant.

Ernest Pike's funeral which took place at Enford almost concurrently with that of his victim was of course a much lower key affair than Crouch's, nevertheless it was dignified and well attended. Curtains were drawn throughout the village as the polished elm coffin was borne on the four wheeled parish bier direct to the graveside to be met by the Enford parish priest, the Reverend Walter Branfoot who officiated jointly with William Keating. The form of service for suicides was by no means unsympathetic; it provided for a choice of psalm from an approved shortlist and the words of the 6th fitted the occasion so perfectly that one imagines it was specifically chosen as a means of passing discreet comment at this sensitive occasion.

"Oh Lord, rebuke me not in thine anger – let all mine enemies be ashamed and sore vexed: let them return and be ashamed suddenly."

It seems that newspaper reporters took the opportunity of speaking to Keating after the funeral, for reports appeared in the national '*Daily Chronicle*' as well as the '*Wiltshire News*' of an interview which gave some inkling of what was to come. Keating referred to a letter which Pike had written to him, and gave extracts from it to the reporters.

"P.C. Pike was intimately known to me for 8 years" the vicar is reported as saying, *"He was a staunch churchman and a Conservative. In my opinion a keener or cleverer policeman did not exist. When the poor fellow went up to Amesbury he was full of hope of being cleared. In my opinion if P.C. Pike could have made a full defence and have called his witnesses, two lives would have been saved and two young families would not have been orphaned."*

The last sentence of this passage outraged Llewellyn.

When the editor of the accurate, but restrained weekly '*Wiltshire Gazette*' saw his competitors' reports in print, he realised he had missed a trick. To recoup lost ground, almost a week later, in the same issue that reported the funerals the paper carried a short article referring to the undercurrents which were starting to stir:

"A number of statements have appeared in the more sensational (halfpenny) pages as to the circumstances leading up to Constable Pike's wild action last week", ran the opening paragraph of the article which went on to explain how the *Gazette* had known of the aspects to the story but did not feel justified in printing them earlier. But the allegations had gained wide currency, reported the article, and so now that they were aware that the Standing Joint Committee were going to consider them at their next meeting on 24th April, they felt justified in publishing the definitive document which embodied all the allegations and complaints. This was a letter written on 9th April by Rev W.W. Keating to the interim Chairman of the S.J.C., Mr H.E. Medlicott

which ran as follows:

"Dear Mr Medlicott,

Will you kindly bring this letter, with P.C. Pike's letter of 31st March to me, before the Standing Joint Committee at their next meeting.

I beg to state in connection with the circumstances of the death of P.C. Pike, of Enford, that the public consider that he was very unfairly dealt with, and that justice should have been granted to him by the Chief Constable, and that he should have been allowed to defend himself against the false charges that were brought against him, and that he should also have been allowed to produce the statements which were made by seven witnesses concerning his innocence. Their names are written in the letter which Pike wrote to me on the night of March 31st. And, further, that the public consider that in such cases as this that the Chief Constable should not have absolute power, but that such cases should be brought before the Standing Joint Committee that they might investigate the case and pass their judgement on it, and that the defaulter should be allowed to defend himself.

I beg to state that this is the fourth case to my knowledge that the Chief Constable acted as he did in Pike's case.

Secondly, I beg to state that the public and Pike's family are very dissatisfied as to the unseemly haste with which the inquest was carried out, as evidence could be brought to bear that there was insanity in Pike's family, which might have affected the verdict, and the jury would have been in a position to bring in a verdict that Pike committed the crime when temporarily insane, which would have allowed the poor widow to get some pension for herself, and her six helpless children, and would have removed the stigma from off Pike's name, viz., that he died a murderer.

Finally, I demand an explanation and an apology such as can be published in the public papers, as to the defamatory remarks which the Chief Constable made concerning me to P.C. Pike at Amesbury on March 31st. His words were: "You have an outside friend, named Rev. Keating, who is no good to you" and "Why should he visit your wife and children and take them for drives?", which statement helped to excite Pike's already excited brain more and more. His words were, "The Chief Constable suggested that there was something between *my wife and you. Now, my wife is a faithful and good-living woman; I cannot stand such a false charge; my brain is going".*

I may add that the Chief Constable knew, for I had told him so some years ago, that I had always taken an interest in the Force, and especially policemen who lived in my parish. P.C. Pike was in my parish for some years. Moreover, I informed the Chief Constable that when I visited Enford I always called to see the Pikes, and I was fond of his children, and sent them for a drive in my governess car. He answered that it was kind of me to do so, and that he was pleased that I took an interest in the Force and did not treat them as machines."

In this letter Keating displayed all the careless hastiness which, despite his obvious passion, characterised his involvement in the case, saying too much about irrelevancies and overlooking important points. He was obviously under the impression that the accusation of murder might have been softened had the inquest jury considered the question of sanity; we know that he was wrong to assume this as it was impossible under the law, though of course *felo de se* could well have been ameliorated. Having dashed this missive off quickly he found it necessary almost immediately to add riders to it, and so he sent two subsequent supplementary letters to Medlicott. The first suggested that the truth of the Three Horse Shoes incident might come out if the police were to initiate a prosecution against Walter Phillimore for harbouring Ernest Pike on the night of 4th March. The second ran as follows:

"I forgot to mention in my letter of 9th inst. That the postscript to P.C. Pike's letter to me of 31st March refers to the time he was lowered by the Chief Constable, which took place four years ago. (Pike was then 1st Class Sergeant at Swindon.)" Keating went on to explain that the charge was one of drunkenness, and concluded his letter, *"I went and told the Chief Constable who it was gave Sgt. Pike the whisky."*

I cannot find a full version of the letter which Ernest wrote to Keating. It may well have been suppressed if the content was considered to be potentially distressing to Mrs Pike. Here though is an extract from it which was published at the time:

Extract from Pike's letter to Keating

"Enford,

Monday, March 31st

Sir,

The Chief Constable has charged me to-day with two offences — (1) that I was in a public house when on duty; (2) that I lied to my superior officer. Let the world know I am not at fault. Make the Chief Constable produce my statements as to my innocence (Pike names the witnesses here), my report, and my wife's, and send them to the Daily Mail, and let the world judge if I am wrong. Crouch is a liar. My brain is going wrong. I love my wife and children very much, and I won't do anything to hurt the hair of their heads. Signed, E. Pike."

In addition to this letter to Keating, Pike had also written two to the London *Daily Mail*, a newspaper in which he seemed to have had pathetic faith. That journal saw fit to publish only one of these. Possibly fearing the prospect of publishing a libel, the *Mail* forwarded the other (which contained names) to the Coroner. Mr Fish, News Editor of the *Mail*, could obviously see the importance of the letter to an inquest, but we do not know whether he was aware as he received and forwarded Pike's notes that he was already too late, and that the inquest proceedings had already been finalised.

(Ernest appears to have written on official notepaper.)

Pike's Letter Published in the Daily Mail 3rd April 1913

"Enford (Station)
Amesbury (Division)
31st March 1913

Sir, I have the honour to report I AM GOING TO SHOOT SERGT. CROUCH TO-NIGHT AND MYSELF.

E. PIKE

(God forgive me, and put strength in my poor wife to bear up; good woman)."

Pike's unpublished Letter to the Daily Mail

"*Sir, I am committing this deed on purpose for the Home Secretary to take the power away from Chief Constables. I have been convicted to-day and not allowed a hearing, which I am not guilty of. The Chief Constable brought a charge against my wife going for a drive with the Rev. Keating. Am I being punished because the Rev Keating told him the rights of my downfall four years ago; then I had all the drinks with Buchanan, Brooks and D.C.C. Robinson. I was told to plead guilty by the D.C.C. and he would help me out of it, which he did not do. This charge to-day is got up by Crouch and Buchanan to give the C.C. the chance to punish me, which he said he would take my stripe away. I hope the Home Secretary will hold a full inquiry into it, and punish the Buchanans and the Chief Constable. I cannot stand it any longer; my poor brain is turning fast. Make the C.C. produce all statements and reports which he would not allow me to know what was put in against me. I don't know what Crouch report contains, nor what Buchanan's said. I know this is all through jealousy.*

Good-bye darling.

E.PIKE

(God forgive me)"

The unbearable strain and mental turmoil felt by Ernest, and the love he felt for Amelia, speaks for itself through these simple and ungrammatical missives, and it is hard to read them even today without a feeling of true pity. Are they indicative of mental imbalance? There is, for sure, opinion in them which may well be mistaken, but there is also assertion that he had not been told what the evidence against him was. If true, they give the lie to Llewellyn's inquest evidence that Crouch and Buchanan were exceptionally fair in what they said at Amesbury. These letters cannot meet the criteria for acceptance as dying declarations, to which English law gave privileged credence, but they would have been of exceptional value to any coroners' jury. Coroner Sylvester was experienced enough to have known that letters are commonly left by suicides. He did not ask any witness at the inquest if they knew of one, and he must have known that the speed with which the inquest was convened would ensure that any letters 'in the pipe-line' would not have had time to surface.

It would be interesting to know exactly where Ernest posted his letters. The old village Post Office was opposite his house, but there was also a small wall mounted box at the crossroads where he was due to meet Crouch. When he left home at 9 p.m. was he so determined that he posted the letters at the Post Office, thus committing himself almost irrevocably, or did he have some doubts of his own resolve and wait to place them in the Coombe box when he was within minutes of committing his desperate last acts?

Perhaps it is possible that he delayed posting them until after he had shot Frank Crouch when he knew he was past all hope of living? We shall never know, but we do know that the last collections of the day were made at 6 p.m. before Ernest had even started to write the letters, so they sat in a post box somewhere in the parish of Enford overnight. It is diverting to speculate that they may have been in the box at Coombe only yards from where the investigations started the following morning, being taken from under the very noses of Archie Buchanan and his men when the box was opened for the 7.55 a.m. collection.[58]

A far more considered complaint than Keating's had also been made. The Enford Parish Council were due to meet routinely on 18th April, but it is a measure of the concern felt in the village that they obviously felt unable to wait until then, and they met in extraordinary session in the school three days earlier, at 7 p.m. on the 15th April, Mr King taking the chair in the absence of the Reverend Branfoot. Mr Lewin Arnold, farmer of West Chisenbury, a former chairman of the council attended by invitation to give advice on procedure. The clerk stated that a letter of acknowledgement had been received from the Chief Constable for the resolution passed in support of Ernest Pike on 10th March — how bitter this must now have sounded to the parish elders — and then the meeting came to its purpose.

---

[58] A Netheravon resident, Percy Stone, born in 1900, stated in 1990 that his sister, who was a servant at Coombe farmhouse, heard the first gunshots and then footsteps which appeared to be those of a man walking to Coombe postbox.

CORRESPONDENCE, FUNERALS, DECISIONS, RESOLUTIONS

There was a belief current in the village that a proper Home Office enquiry was to be put in motion and it was felt that any terms of reference should therefore be carefully drawn up. Consequently, another Parish Council resolution calling for full investigation into the circumstances leading up to and immediately following the death of Police Constable Pike was now unanimously approved, making specific reference to the following points:

1. With what breach of discipline had Pike been charged leading to the Amesbury hearing?
2. Why was the inquest pressed with such haste?
3. Why did the Coroner inform his jury that they must not consider the state of Pike's mind?
4. Pikes relatives had no opportunity of being represented at the inquest. Had they been, they could have given important evidence of insanity in the family.

The day after this resolution was passed by the Enford Parish Council, the two mysterious men who had arrived at Coombe by motor car just as the proceedings were closing also wrote to Mr Medlicott.

"*Malmesbury, Wilts; 16th April, 1913*

Dear Sir,

Will you allow us, on behalf of ourselves and the other relatives of the late Police Constable Ernest Pike, and his widow, to appeal to you for further inquiry to be made into the charge made against him, and on account of which he was degraded. We have a copy of the statement which we believe was sent to the Chief Constable (a copy of which we send to you) in which Pike asserted his innocence of the charge made against him. We would especially draw your attention to the fact that Pike states that Sergeant Crouch came to him when standing outside the Three Horse Shoes and said, "Didn't I hear you come out of that house just now?" Pike replied "Certainly not." The sergeant said "I will know," and went across to the public house and inquired, and we believe both the landlord and his wife and their son told him Pike had not been in the house. It appears, therefore, if Pike's account is correct, that the sergeant did not see Pike come out of the house, but heard someone come out, and as the landlord's son was standing outside the front door under the verandah when the sergeant reached the door it is possible the evidence of some of the witnesses proffered would have proved it was he and not Pike whom the sergeant heard come out of the house. It was evidently a dark rough night and the sergeant might easily have been deceived.

Again, if Pike had been in the public house in the course of his duty why should he be punished; and why, in any case, should not the evidence of the landlord, his wife and son, and others, have been laid before the Chief Constable? If Pike was there, not in the course of his duty, why was not the publican punished for harbouring him? Pike had been in the service for 18 years, and had on more than one occasion been commended, and once received £5 by order of the judge for his special service. At the inquest his character was well reported, and yet he was condemned on the sole evidence of the sergeant, as against his own evidence and that of several witnesses.

We contend, sir, that the hearing, if it can be called one, was conducted most unfairly, and that there is a very strong ground for inquiry and a possible reversal of the sentence.

Whether Pike was guilty or not, and especially if he was innocent, the very injustice of the procedure to him, and the heavy sentence, was sufficient to unhinge the mind of a man having a tendency to insanity. The widow stated at the inquest that he returned home from Amesbury at about 6 o'clock in a depressed state of mind, and almost broken-hearted, and stayed in the room all by himself until he went out at 9 o'clock. After such a terrible harassing experience he had to go on duty again at 9 o'clock and to meet Sergeant Crouch at or about 11.

We feel that there is just cause for complaint in relation to the Coroner's inquest in view of the serious effect the verdict must have on the future of the widow and children. The body was found at about 11 a.m. and the inquest was held the same afternoon at 3.30. The widow only received notice to attend the inquest at about 2.45 and lived a mile away. She thus had no opportunity to obtain advice or assistance, and we ourselves could not reach the inquest in time. At 1.15 we were informed of the death, but not of the time of the inquest. As speedily as possible we motored from Malmesbury to Enford, a distance of 32 miles. We

CORRESPONDENCE, FUNERALS, DECISIONS, RESOLUTIONS

called at the widow's house at about 4.40 o'clock and found she had gone to the inquest. We at once motored there and on our arrival the Coroner was just closing the enquiry.

The verdict, in the absence of evidence which would have had a bearing on Pike's probable mental condition, was one which had the effect of depriving deceased's widow and six young children of the pension to which his eighteen years of faithful service would have entitled them. Had we an opportunity of attending the inquest we could have proved that the deceased's mother, immediately after his birth, had so severe an attack of puerperal fever that she was taken to a lunatic asylum, and that up to the present time she suffers from extreme depression. Again, on deceased's father's side his (the deceased's) first cousin, Charles Pike, was insane and died in a lunatic asylum, and Charles Pike's sister was also insane.

Pike's letter to his former vicar, Rev Keating, in which he said, "I can't stand it; it is turning my brain," is an indication of the state of mind, and shows he was not fit to go on duty after so harassing an experience.

It is evident that the state of his mind was not taken into consideration, as the Coroner told a member of the jury it was not part of their duty to inquire into it. Had an opportunity been given for the jury to do so it might have prevented the great hardship caused to the widow and children.

May we most respectfully urge you to do all that is possible to get this verdict amended in their interest.

We are, sir, yours obediently,

JAMES HANKS, Father of the widow of P.C. Pike

T.H. MORSE, Husband of P.C. Pike's sister."

It is interesting to note that some relatives on the Crouch side also found out only by chance what had happened. Mrs Hoare, wife of the licensee of The Lion and Fiddle at Hilperton near Trowbridge, became aware of the tragedy affecting her sister, Kate Crouch, through overhearing a conversation between customers on Tuesday 1st April. She at once left for Netheravon.

In addition to the local furore, the columns of the *Police Review* were full, week by week, of editorial comment and anonymous letters referring to the case. There had long been criticism of ex-military Chief Constables and the 'One Man System' of control in county forces, with unspecified warnings of disaster if these things were not changed. Now that those predictions had come to pass in bloody and spectacular fashion, Llewellyn, to his great discomfiture, had become a source of justification for the doom-laden prognostications of the amateur oracles whose writings filled the pages of the magazine.

Llewellyn was outraged by the adverse comment, wherever it appeared, but he naturally felt the *Police Review* copy particularly keenly, as this nationally distributed magazine was widely read by policemen including his own subordinates. Barbed comment flew from both sides as soon as news of the shootings became known, although not until some weeks later was a sharp personal correspondence between Llewellyn and Kempster published in which the editor of the *Police Review* complained that the Chief had made unfounded accusations against the magazine's reporting of some aspects of the case. It sounded like the preliminary to an action for libel, but the matter subsided without recourse to law.

By mid-April there was far too much concern abroad to be simply ignored by the Wiltshire Police authorities. A full independent Home Office inquiry would not be at all welcome to them, but an inquiry held under their own auspices, totally within their own control, might silence criticism especially if some ground were to be conceded as a sop to the families and other complainants without incriminating any senior policemen

The Standing Joint Committee met at Trowbridge on 24th April and one of the first agenda items was to appoint the Earl of Radnor to the vacant chair, after which the Chief Constable formally reported the deaths to him. The details of a pension for Mrs Crouch had been agreed a week earlier at a meeting of the Accounts subcommittee (which was comprised of members of the S.J.C., including the Chairman and Vice Chairman) and Llewellyn endorsed this carefully to the S.J.C. specifying the individual amounts payable in respect of the widow and each of her two young sons.

As for Mrs Pike, Llewellyn made no recommendations, simply referring the committee to 'section 2 of the Police Act 1890'. He did not explain what this laid down, and it is unlikely that many of the committee knew without any explanation, but more importantly perhaps, the public reading the newspaper reports of the meeting would have had no idea either. Had they done so there may have been concern expressed, for what this section provided for was that the widow of a policeman who had died from any cause other than an injury received on duty *might* be paid a single gratuity *but only if the Standing Joint Committee thought fit*. What they now thought fit was to postpone any decision on payment to the widow and six children pending further inquiry, consoling themselves with the thought that Mrs Pike's immediate needs were being met by her family and also from the proceeds of a fund which they knew had been set up by Keating.

Moving on, the Chief Constable formally asked that a full investigation be made into the whole affair, in view of what had appeared in the press, and this was acceded to.

Enter Reuben George

Mr Reuben George, County Councillor for Swindon North, was a new member of the S.J.C. and a man of the people, very different from the magistrates who held sway within the Committee. A Gloucestershire born Quaker and sometime Methodist, who whenever one sees his name mentioned it is associated with worthy causes, often lost ones – he it would be who would unsuccessfully support the move to remove the appointment fee for county magistrates. George now saw that something was wrong in the way the system was handling the Pike affair and he asked the new chairman whether there were going to be any legal difficulties in assisting the widow of the constable. His concern was shared by Baptist minister Rev H.B. Bardwell, another new and non-magisterial S.J.C. member who seems to have been well intentioned but slightly out of touch with worldly matters. Radnor's reply about financial relief was non-committal, but what he then had to say should have set alarm bells ringing wherever justice was honoured. He proposed to leave the matter of the inquiry requested by Llewellyn until the end of the meeting when the committee could withdraw from public and press scrutiny, and discuss in private the course to be adopted. *"Whenever there is anything tending to the discredit of the police the reporters are asked to leave and publicity is shunned"* had said the *Salisbury Times* in September 1901.

Twelve years later nothing had changed.

After some hours Radnor emerged to advise the waiting pressmen that a public inquiry would be held under the auspices of the Standing Joint Committee at Devizes on Thursday 8th May. Three Justices of the Peace had been appointed to form a sub-committee; Sir John Tankerville Goldney, Mr Henry Edmonstone Medlicott and Mr Francis Reynolds Yonge Radcliffe K.C.

Chapter 8

The Sort of Court

The Public Inquiry
Devizes, 10.30 a.m. Thursday 8th May 1913

At 10.30 in the morning of 8th May the interested parties assembled in the Assize Courtroom at Devizes for the opening of proceedings. All three commissioners were lawyers. Radcliffe, who was to be the chairman of the Inquiry was born in 1851 and had taken Silk in 1904. From 1887 to 1904 he had been Recorder of Devizes, leaving that post to become Recorder of Portsmouth, a post he would hold until 1914.[59] Medlicott had been called to the Bar of Middle Temple in 1866, and Goldney, having been called by Inner Temple in 1869 had practised in Liverpool before going on to have a distinguished career in the Colonial Judiciary, having finally been Chief Justice of Trinidad between 1892 and 1902. The Clerk to the S.J.C., Mr W.L. Bown was also present to do duty as thought fit.

Despite being presided over by an eminent K.C. in the imposing surroundings of an Assize Courtroom, the inquiry proved to be a ramshackle affair. It was being held under the auspices of a comparatively lowly body, the S.J.C. which was only a County Council committee, and there was no power to compel attendance by witnesses. Evidence was not given on oath, and Radcliffe set the uncertain tone early in the proceedings by making a woolly declaration that they were "*a sort of court of investigation*". Although the Chief Constable and the Pike family were legally represented, William Keating was allowed to take a seat at the lawyers table and was permitted to examine witnesses and to address the tribunal on his own behalf. In opening the proceedings Radcliffe said that the points of the Enford Parish Council resolution of 15th April were the basis for the inquiry, but there was no evidence or statement given

---

[59] A recorder was a barrister appointed to preside over Borough Quarter Sessions.

119

on their behalf, and it was Keating who assumed the mantle of keeper of the public conscience.

Allowing him to do so would have been a clever move by the Chief Constable's friends, for despite his good intentions the Wilsford vicar was given to thoughtlessness and injudicious comment which did him and his case no good. Llewellyn's party surely knew before they came

Plate k: Pike Family

to court that they would be able to convincingly undermine the clergyman's credibility, and Keating was to oblige his detractors handsomely, by drifting from the core issues, failing to conform with basic inquiry procedure, and then subsequently having to apologise for it.

He may well have been putting forward widely held concerns, but once the proceedings commenced Ernest Pike's family and friends might have been forgiven for thinking that the clergyman did more harm than good for their cause. The Wilsford vicar was a poor advocate, excitable and indistinct, and he also had a personal agenda, believing that he had to clear his own name of the suggestion of impropriety with Mrs Pike; the rage he felt at this suggestion made him appear to be an implacable enemy of Llewellyn.

This was to the advantage of the Chief Constable, because uncomfortable criticism by Keating, even if true, could be explained away as personal antipathy. The more outrageous and unreliable Keating could be made to appear the better it would be to divert serious and expert scrutiny of the troublesome aspects of the case. Perhaps his own clerical colleagues knew of his headstrong attitudes, and decided to keep an eye on him, for three senior clergymen were also present as members of the public and they sat themselves down in the Grand Jury box. Canon Arthur Barugh Thynne, vicar of nearby Seend, had been curate in Keating's parish of Wilsford over forty years earlier. His son-in-law, the Reverend Gilbert King was vicar of Easterton which neighboured Wilsford and his vicarage was to become one of many focal points for collections on behalf of Mrs Pike and her children. The other clergyman present was W.H. Kewley, vicar of Potterne another nearby parish where Medlicott was a prominent member of the congregation.

Titley Rides Again

The Chief Constable had engaged Mr Titley of Bath as solicitor. He has appeared in these pages before, as Pike's solicitor in 1901. He in turn instructed Mr T. H. Parr, barrister. Pike's relatives were represented by Mr A.G. Smith, a Melksham solicitor. Ernest's in-laws, the Hanks, seem to have taken a more prominent position than the Pikes, reflecting their concern for Amelia. Ernest's youngest sister, 30 year old Alice was the last of his siblings to be resident in Malmesbury and it was her husband, Thomas Henry Morse who had loyally joined forces with Amelia's father to try and reach the inquest and both men then authored the explicit letter to Mr Medlicott which had been reprinted in the *Wiltshire Gazette*.

There was a large contingent of policemen all ready to give evidence of one sort or another, and it became clear as the inquiry proceeded that many were there in anticipation of questions about events not related to the Pike case.

Mr Radcliffe opened the inquiry. Given that a particular result was required by the authorities, he was in a difficult position, but he tried to lend an air of impartiality. It will be remembered that the Enford Council Resolution (which Radcliffe now said was the basis of the present Inquiry) listed four points:

- What was the breach of discipline leading to Ernest Pike's appearance before the Chief Constable at Amesbury on 31st March?
- Why was the inquest pressed on with such haste?
- Why did the coroner refuse to allow the jury to consider Ernest Pike's state of mind?
- Why were the Pike family prevented from giving evidence?

The way in which things were going to be handled was quickly made clear when Radcliffe immediately disposed of three of these points or perhaps, using his flexible standards, he 'sort of' disposed of them, for he eventually allowed questioning to drift into matters he had initially ruled out of court.

What he said in opening the proceedings was that the inquiry was not going to inquire into the timing of the inquest or the coroner's summing up. The coroner was a gentleman of great experience said Radcliffe superfluously, and went on to declare that as far as the present inquiry was concerned it did not matter to them whether the coroner acted hastily or not.

But if he intended to show that he supported the coroner absolutely Radcliffe then backtracked; although the inquest itself would not be up for discussion, he *was* prepared to allow discussion of the mental state of Pike, because there was, he said, a bare possibility that the Standing Joint Committee might consider it appropriate to award a gratuity to the dead constable's widow. They might act differently *if they thought the dead man was innocent!* This was an astounding thing to say for Pike could only be innocent of *felo de se* if it was accepted that he was insane when he committed suicide, and the authority for overturning an inquest verdict lay with the Kings Bench Division of the High Court.

By Radcliffe's guidelines, all that was left of the Enford Resolution was for the Chief Constable's actions in connection with the disciplinary hearing at Amesbury to be inquired into. At least the Chief could properly be questioned by this inquiry run by his masters of the Standing Joint Committee couldn't he? Well, if he could this particular inquiry wasn't going to do it. The right to raise questions relating to the so called 'One Man System' was now ruled out of order by Radcliffe with the excuse that as Chief Constables' powers were set by Parliament, and as there was a Police Act Amendment Bill currently before the House of Commons, the inquiry would make no comment on the police disciplinary system.

Refusal to discuss the matter on these grounds was spurious; Parliamentary debate did not render a subject *sub judice*, and the contents of the Bill were being openly discussed in the press.

What was the point of setting up an inquiry which immediately declared that it could not, or would not look into nearly all of the complaints which it had been ostensibly convened to investigate? The answer has to be that it was set in motion in order to preclude any inquiry being made by any authority from outside the county, to pay lip service to propriety, and to exonerate the officials involved, principally Llewellyn. The Chief Constable had himself asked for an inquiry in order to clear his name of any sort of allegations, and the proceedings were quite clearly aimed at providing him with the opportunity to do so. It is not hard to imagine the frustration and suspicions of the Pikes, Hanks and Keating, having thought that they had forced an inquiry into the failings of the inquest and 'One Man System' to be told at the outset that this was not going to be done.

By the time the sub-committee had ruled out all the things it felt unable to do, there wasn't a great deal left of the original complaints, but Mr Radcliffe said that the matter which *concerned the S.J.C. most* was that of whether the Amesbury hearing was properly conducted.

He is not on record as considering which matters most concerned anybody else in the court room other than making an allusion to Keating, whom he noted was in court. There was a *"side issue"*, said Radcliffe coyly, and he did not see how they could keep off it. He meant the issue of Keating's friendship with the Pikes, and the allegations flowing from it. Keating wanted these allegations refuted, and Llewellyn was keen to have it accepted that he had never made them, and so each man was seeking an apology from the other.

The investigation into the propriety of what happened at Amesbury could have been done without any further consideration of whether Pike was actually guilty or not of having been in the Three Horse Shoes. That really did not matter, for it was the process rather than the facts of the case which should have been at question. The real questions were, did the evidence justify charges being brought against Pike, and once they were, did the police hold a proper, fair and just examination, and come to a conclusion based on the evidence? Predictably though, the proceedings became a casual re-trial of Ernest Pike and it now seemed to be accepted that if he were once again 'found guilty' of the Three Horse Shoes business then the ends would justify the means insofar as police behaviour was concerned.

Although much was to be made of Ernest's disciplinary record, the Race Plain incident was never once mentioned, rightly so, for he was entitled to be considered innocent in that case. Llewellyn and the commissioners were ready enough though, to dwell on other old and irrelevant cases involving other policemen which Keating had unwisely brought up. These were easy to refute and conveniently obscured the central issues of the Pike affair.

The Game's Afoot

Smith opened for the family: He was careful — he did not want to cast aspersions on the Chief Constable, he said, but surely a mistake had been made by somebody? The purpose of the Amesbury hearing was not simply to punish Pike, it was for getting at the truth. Perhaps Crouch *had* believed to the best of his opinion that Pike was guilty as charged, but the evidence the sergeant presented was far too flimsy for the Chief Constable to take action upon. Smith accepted that the matters relating to the conduct of the inquest were beyond the jurisdiction of the inquiry. He would, however, bring evidence relating to the possibility of Ernest Pike's mind being temporarily off balance.

Parr for Llewellyn: The Chief Constable welcomed the inquiry, after all, was it not he who had asked for it to be held? Hurrah then, might we say for the Chief, but there were no cheers recorded in court – in fact the only man who would draw applause, despite his extravagance of style, would be Keating.

Wasting no time in going for the clergyman, Barrister Parr implicitly emphasised the matters that his client really felt to be important. Serious imputations, he said, which obviously emanated from Mr Keating, had been made in the press against his client, both personally and against the office which he held. The Chief Constable would defend his personal honour in the usual way in the usual court, said Parr – an unsubtle threat of libel action – but he felt he had to defend that of his official position before this inquiry. *He* would not rush into print like Keating had done.

Llewellyn in the Box

Llewellyn entered the witness box – he would be there for over an hour – and the versions of the events of two months earlier at the Three Horse Shoes were once again trotted out. The Chief said that he had seen all seven statements offered in support of Pike, but he had disregarded them. What convinced him of the truth of the charge was the good demeanour of Crouch, as opposed to bluster from Pike.

No one pressed him to explain why, if he had kept an open mind until he was able to compare the demeanour of the two men, he had dismissed Pike's witness statements in advance of the hearing. The seven statements were produced, Llewellyn confirming that all except one were in Pike's handwriting. The barrister carefully pointed out that no written statement had been made by landlord Walter Phillimore, but he asked the Chief what action he took in respect of the statements from Emma and Thomas, direct evidence from two witnesses emphatically declaring that Pike had not been in the public house. Llewellyn's response was "*I put them aside as being biased, because the witnesses might be implicated*".[60] The hatchet job continued when the specious casuistry of holding out Pike's failure to recognise two strangers, and his second visit to Chisenbury, as some sort of evidence of guilt was repeated by the Chief Constable without apparent embarrassment.

Pike, it will be recalled, both in his suicide notes and in conversation with Amelia, stated that he was not allowed to bring his evidence, and that he was not told what Crouch and Buchanan's reports said, but unsurprisingly Llewellyn's story, supported by the two Buchanans was much different on this point. It is easy to see why Llewellyn and the Buchanans should lie; they had futures, careers, reputations to guard. But why should Ernest have been so adamant in his last declarations unless he was telling the truth? It could perhaps be put down to mental imbalance, but then what price Coroner Sylvester's summing up and imperious exclusion of this possibility?

Llewellyn mentioned the Phillimore *alibi*, and again rejected it out of hand, not because of any intrinsic flaw in the evidence, but simply because he was not prepared to believe anything the publican said. He made a slip which should have been seized upon later in his cross examination by Smith, but which, like so many other things was unaccountably overlooked when the time came.

Asked by Parr if Pike's manner at the Amesbury hearing had been convincing, the Chief said, "*No, I formed the opinion that he was lying, not with regard to Chisenbury, but with regard to being in the public house.*" The entire point about the visit to Chisenbury was of course that Pike could not have been there at 9.55 *and* in the Three Horse Shoes at 10 p.m., that being the time from which Crouch claimed to have had it under observation. (Radcliffe interjected to ask exactly how far it was from

---

[60] Under law then extant, no person should have been excluded from giving evidence even if they stood to lose or gain by the result of the trial: Evidence Act 1843.

Chisenbury to the Three Horse Shoes, and the surprisingly accurate answer, "*About 1,570 yards,*" confirmed the point).

And so if the Chief did not disbelieve Pike's claim to have been in Chisenbury, and did not disbelieve (he said that he didn't) the evidence of the *Swan* customers who saw Pike heading that way at 9.30, then he had no reason to disbelieve Pike's claim to have been there when he said he was. How then could Llewellyn find Pike guilty of being in the Three Horse Shoes almost concurrently?

Llewellyn's statements would get less believable before the day was out, but the worst part about the proceedings is that he was never seriously challenged over the obvious discrepancies in his testimony. It is quite easy to play 'what if' games with what passes for evidence in the Three Horse Shoes affair, but whatever construction is put on the various statements, and whatever sympathies or opinions may be held, it is blindingly obvious that there were far too many inconsistencies for the Chief Constable to fairly come to a decision based, as it would seem, solely on the comparative demeanours of the deceased men.

The Pike's relationship with Keating was raised as a question, and it was now that the Chief admitted that he thought it his duty to stop it, though he had never had any detrimental reports about it until November 1912 when Archibald Buchanan arrived in Amesbury. He confirmed that the selection of Colerne as Pike's next duty station was influenced by the need, as he saw it, to put distance between the constable and the clergyman. Parr then put in two documents, the first detailing Pike's record, for better and for worse. The subject of the 1909 Swindon Baths escapade, and Keating's part in questioning the severity of the punishment, was raised, which turned attention to the second piece of paper, this charge report:

CHARGE AND DATES	DEFENCE
Being drunk at the Baths while on night duty, and also conduct unbecoming a police officer, thereby bringing discredit upon the police force. Feb 10th 1909.	Sir, On this particular night it was very cold, and I was tempted to have a drop of whisky, which I am not used to, so very little overcame me. I am very sorry for what happened, and I promise to refrain from all intoxicating liquor for the future. I most respectfully ask the Chief Constable to give me another chance, and I will endeavour to rub out this black mark.

Llewellyn now said that the offence would normally have meant dismissal. Perhaps Superintendent Thomas J. Robinson's mitigating plea on the report had worked to a limited extent:

"*This man has been a good officer, and has done his work well up to now. He knows well how to handle a case, and to get the necessary evidence together, and I am very sorry indeed to see him in this mess. He has a good wife and five young children. I hope you will not reduce him to a constable. Give him another chance and remove him,* (i.e. relocate him) *and I think you will not regret it. He is very penitent now. I hope I may respectfully appeal to you not to reduce him to a constable.*

T.J. ROBINSON, D.C.C."

Pike had claimed in his suicide note that Robinson had not helped him in this matter, but this note shows that the Superintendent did at least try.

Parr then moved on to the subject of adverse criticism which had appeared in the press, and Llewellyn, whilst blaming Keating for starting it all, singled out the *Police Review* as a particular thorn in his side. He complained that it was intolerable that he should be criticised without the opportunity of replying, a particularly arrogant comment when one considers how little right of reply was afforded by the 'one-man system' he so vigorously defended.

The questions of whether Pike might have been legitimately inside the public house and whether the publican should have been prosecuted for harbouring were now raised. Pike had always said that he was not in the pub, legitimately or otherwise, so that quite scotched the first suggestion. The point about prosecuting Phillimore was that Keating and the family took the view that the failure by the police to do so was a tacit admission that they had no belief in their own case, and that they dare not see it tested before a court. This risky tactic by the Pike supporters was nevertheless nimbly side stepped by Llewellyn who said that prosecution of the publican was impossible because Pike had killed the only witness. He meant the only *prosecution* witness of course.

Keating Gets it Wrong (Part 1)

Llewellyn now raised a matter which should have been ruled out of court, telling the inquiry that he had written to Keating on 15th April, asking for the names of the other policemen whom Keating had alleged to have been similarly harshly treated by him. Keating, at the lawyers table knew embarrassment was looming for him, and was agitated into asking Radcliffe if he might say something. The chairman would not stop the Chief Constable though, replying to Keating's request in the following words:

"Yes, but you had better say it later on."

The reason for the clergyman's discomfiture soon became apparent, for his accusations concerning the other cases, which were utterly irrelevant to the matter in hand anyway, were disposed of embarrassingly quickly. Conveniently, those policemen still serving who had been involved in the cases mentioned were in the courtroom, suitably indignant that their names had been raised in this way.

Keating had no doubt seen that this was coming and had spoken up in order to withdraw his allegations. He should have been permitted to do so, but it seems that Radcliffe and Llewellyn wanted the satisfaction of showing him up as an unreliable complainant.

THE SORT OF COURT

If Radcliffe could open the inquiry by ruling out discussion of the coroner's actions and of the police disciplinary system, why could he not have similarly stated that these complaints of Keating's were similarly beyond the scope of the proceedings and ruled those out too? One of the incidents had in fact occurred during Sterne's period of command, and so could hardly be used against Llewellyn. This could have been pointed out to Keating in advance to give him the opportunity to drop the matter and save the Inquiry's time. Keating had badly damaged his own credibility, and Llewellyn's and Radcliffe's manipulative strategy ensured the maximum damage was caused.

Parr is allowed to Get Away with Introducing a Taboo Subject.....

Quite unbelievably, in view of the guidelines set by the sub-committee, Parr now raised the questions of criticism about the inquest, which the Chairman had ruled out of order at the very beginning of the inquiry. Why no member of the sub-committee, all experienced lawyers remember, called Parr to order is yet another suspicious mystery. Were they simply going to allow the Chief Constable and his barrister to introduce anything that suited them? Keating and Smith could not easily raise a point of order though, for they themselves had wanted these matters raised.

On the matter of haste, Llewellyn confirmed that he had been the person who first informed the coroner of the Coombe incident. He had given an outline of the case, and told Mr Sylvester that *"it would suit my convenience if he could hold the inquest that day rather than next"*. Obviously the Chief Constable's convenience was a matter of the utmost importance to Sylvester.

Llewellyn said in answer to Parr's prompting that he had seen Mrs Pike in the morning of 1st April when he called at her house on the way to Coombe. She had not, he said, made any requests concerning a postponement of the inquest or calling any relatives. (Of course she hadn't asked for a postponement. What grounds could she have had for doing so? At the time Llewellyn called she did not yet know that her husband was dead. Nobody did. Armed police were still out looking for Ernest!).

Moving on to the matter of Pike's mental state, Llewellyn said that he would have called for an adjournment of the inquest had he had any suspicion of insanity. Such a verdict, he said rather sickeningly, he would have welcomed, as it would have lessened the slur on the force. In response to a final question during his examination-in-chief, he stated that he had known nothing of the two men from Malmesbury who had been trying to reach the inquest.

.... and Smith Punishes the Chief Constable for It

Smith rose to cross-examine. Radcliffe had said that discussion of Pike's mental state might be discussed, but Parr had led the Chief Constable beyond this with his questions about the haste of the inquest and a possible adjournment. This provided Smith with one wonderful opportunity which he took.

In good lawyers fashion he got Llewellyn talking by asking him some easy, sympathetic questions about the heavy burden of responsibility of a Chief Constables lot. "*Oh, yes*", chirped the man in the box, "*very heavy burden of responsibility*". Smith confirmed with the Chief, quite innocuously, that there was no means of appeal against his disciplinary decisions. Then he struck. He asked Llewellyn if he had heard Mr Foreman Tilley's question to the coroner about whether the inquest jury were to consider Pike's state of mind.

If he saw what was coming Llewellyn might now have regretted Parr's unchallenged introduction of the subject. He wriggled. He blustered. Just the sort of behaviour that he said had "proved to his satisfaction" that Ernest was lying at the Amesbury hearing.

As you read the following dialogue, remember that Llewellyn had placed himself in a seat next to the coroner at the inquest and that Mr Sylvester had no problem hearing what was said by the foreman of the jury in the small room used for the inquest, nor did any of the reporters whose newspapers all carried the account of that simple exchange between Tilley and Sylvester, "*Are we to consider the state of Pike's mind?*" — "*Not in such a case as this*".

Smith's opening question indicates his surprise that the matter of the inquest is open for discussion at all.

Smith: "*With regard now to this question of the inquest, I shall take it now, as it was dealt with late in your examination in chief. You were present all the time?*"

Llewellyn: "*Yes, and I gave evidence.*"

Smith: "*Did you hear the foreman of the jury suggest that some consideration might be given to the state of Pike's mind?*"

Llewellyn: "*He made some communication to the Coroner, the exact text of which I cannot remember.*"

Smith: "*There was a suggestion that Pike's sanity should be considered?*"

Llewellyn: "*I don't think it was put in that way; the state of his mind at the time of the deed; it might have been*".

Smith: "*In the Wiltshire Gazette for April 3rd — and I may say reports in that paper are generally very accurate — it states: 'Before leaving the Court the foreman asked the Coroner if it was any part of the duty of the jury to consider the state of Pike's mind.'*"

Llewellyn: "*That is a question for the Coroner, not myself*".

Smith: "*Did you hear it said?*"

Llewellyn: "*I did not hear the exact question. I should not like to mention 'aye' or 'nay' to it. There was no intimation to me at the time of the inquest as to that question, and I do not know what was in their minds.*"

Smith: "*Surely you would know if the question was asked?*"

Llewellyn: "*I cannot say 'Yes' or 'No', I do not know the exact words*".

Smith: "*There was a question to Pike's sanity?*"

Llewellyn: "*There was a question asked by the foreman: I will not say it was that question.*"

Smith could see that he had done enough and would get no further. He was not getting any help from Radcliffe who might, if truly impartial, have pressed the Chief Constable to come clean, so he wrapped up the matter with one final question which Llewellyn answered unsatisfactorily:

Smith: "*You did not consider that of sufficient importance to justify you in asking for an adjournment to go into the question of sanity?*"

Llewellyn: "*That would be in the Coroner's discretion.*"

The significance of this embarrassing passage-at-arms is clear – Llewellyn did not want to tell the truth. Having earlier said that he would have welcomed an insanity verdict "*to lessen the slur on the force*", and would have asked for an adjournment if the question had been raised, he could not now admit that he had heard the foreman raising it, though it is obvious that he must have heard. (Mr Tilley, the foreman, kept away from the inquiry, as did Coroner Sylvester)

A Descent into Sarcasm

Mr Smith now moved to the events of 4th March in Enford, asking about the nature of Ernest's regular duties around the parish. He got the Chief Constable to admit that it was quite reasonable for the constable to have visited Chisenbury for a second time. When asked how long it would take Pike to walk between the public houses in his patch in order to see them closed, the man who knew the distance to the exact yard when answering a friendly advocate opined that it was a difficult question to answer. Mr Smith helped him; would it take an hour?

"*I cannot say*", said Llewellyn, "*It might take him five.*"

"*Well,*" said Smith, "*I suppose that it might if he crawled round on his hands and knees.*"

A memorable scene in the 1960s film of Keith Waterhouse's book 'Billy Liar' shows the eponymous hero daydreaming about mowing down irritating questioners with a tommy gun. It is not hard to imagine Llewellyn, the old Maxim Gun commander from

Matabeleland now eyeing Mr Smith and fantasising in much the same way, even though a better advocate than Smith would have made mincemeat of Llewellyn over the string of inconsistencies in his evidence.

The subject of the Walter Phillimore's *alibi* evidence was raised, and the Chief trotted out the line about putting it aside because it was biased, and could not be considered. Smith, no doubt better aware of the Evidence Act, pointedly disagreed. Of course it could have been biased, any evidence can be, and Llewellyn was entitled to fairly weigh its credibility, but, pointed out Smith, witness was quite wrong to say that it could *not be considered*. Pike had a right to have his evidence heard. *Rat-tat-tat-tat-tat!*

Llewellyn's confidence was no doubt shaken by Smith but not his arrogance, for when the solicitor asked the Chief Constable if he had asked Walter Phillimore to come to give evidence at Amesbury, he expostulated

"*Certainly not!*"
"*Nor the wife nor the son?*"

"*Certainly not! Crouch's evidence,*" crooned the Chief without a whiff of shame at the virtual lunacy of what he was saying, '*was overwhelming*'.

Below Parr

Smith wasn't the man the Chief really loved to hate though. That honour was reserved for William Keating, and Smith found it necessary to cool the temperature by remarking that the complaints which had led to the inquiry had not only been made by Mr Keating, but by members of the Pike family too (and, he should have added, the Enford Parish Council). Chairman Radcliffe remembered the Hanks/Morse letter and piped up:

"*There was a letter from them in the papers about it*".

"*It should be read out now!*", thundered Keating from his seat at the lawyers table.

Mr Parr was embarrassed. He had not known about this letter, despite it being quite firmly in the public domain by virtue of publication in the *Wiltshire Gazette* in April. "*I should have read that*", he said ruefully.

Moving along, the wisdom of allowing the two men to meet late at night in a remote spot after the afternoon *fracas* between them was questioned. In reply to Smith's implied suggestion that it was unwise, Llewellyn answered,

"*It was the last thing I should have thought of.*"

Keating gets it Wrong (Part 2)

The relationship between Llewellyn and Keating was like that between two terriers asked to share one bone. The Chief Constable was particularly incensed by Keating's suggestions in the newspapers that his attitude to his men and his powers as Chief Constable had now caused the loss of two lives. He also affected to resent the suggestion that he had made allusion to a relationship between Keating and Mrs Pike. For his part, the clergyman was outraged not only by the wrongs done to Ernest Pike, but also by his belief that Llewellyn *had* made the scandalous remarks.

As Smith's cross-examination of Llewellyn closed, Radcliffe asked Keating if he wished to ask any questions whilst witness was still in the box. True to form the garrulous vicar seemed incapable of differentiating between a question and a statement and Radcliffe had to stop him burbling, and ask him to confine himself to interrogation. Keating continued in the same declamatory vein though, but before Radcliffe could tug on his leash, Llewellyn started to bark back. Whenever the great man or his barrister spoke, this seems to have been the signal throughout the inquiry for the commissioners not to intervene, so the Chief took the uninterrupted opportunity to absolutely deny making any suggestions of impropriety involving Keating and Amelia Pike.

Llewellyn stood down, and both Buchanans then gave supporting evidence about the care with which, they said, their Chief Constable had prepared for the Amesbury hearing. Predictable enough this may have been, but it highlights the point that if care was indeed taken then the inconsistencies in the accounts of the Three Horse Shoes incident were either incompetently overlooked by Llewellyn, or were deliberately and corruptly ignored by him.

Pike's letter to the *Daily Mail* which had been redirected to the coroner was now produced, and its contents made public for the first time, as a result of which the Chairman thought he should call Superintendent Thomas J. Robinson, the Deputy Chief Constable, to challenge those parts of it relating to the 1909 Swindon Baths incident. The tall ex-Guardsman denied that he had then advised Pike to plead guilty. Keating now complained that the Superintendent should have stopped Archie Buchanan, then an inspector, giving Pike whisky and found himself the butt of laughter when Robinson said, with barbed sarcasm:

"*Even if you had come in we might have offered you a glass.*"

"*Well, it was wrong to give drink to officers on duty,*" said the piqued Keating, obviously unconvinced that no fault lay with Buchanan.

Superintendent Brooks now took the stand. When he was asked to explain why he had stood by and watched whilst an inspector gave strong liquor to a sergeant on duty, he said:

"*We were in our own house, so to speak, not in a public house or the street.*"

Anxious to score a point somewhere, Keating pettily asked if the function had been properly licensed for the sale of alcohol. It was, said Brooks, and Keating's irrelevant attempt at trouble making can hardly have done his cause much good.

Dignity returned to the proceedings when Amelia Pike was called to give her evidence, confirming what had been said in her father's letter to Medlicott. She explained that she would have testified to the inquest about insanity in the Pike family, but that the coroner had told her just to answer questions that were put to her. She also told of the forty minutes notice that she had been given to attend the inquest. It was at that point, she said, that she asked her relatives to attend, though they had in fact pre-empted her request and were already on their way, having set off as soon as they heard the news of Ernest's death. She then stood down.

What happened next during Walter Phillimore's examination tested the confidence of those who wanted to believe in Pike's innocence of the Three Horse Shoes' affair.

Walter on the Spot

Phillimore gave his evidence that he had seen the constable at Chisenbury on 4th March at 9.55 p.m. and that they had exchanged greetings. He further claimed to have told this to Buchanan on 5th March.

Mr Parr must have noticed that the first recorded reference to the Chisenbury meeting was not made until Ernest Pike wrote his statement on 12th March. He saw a weakness and rose to cross-examine with a purpose:

"*Do you really say, Mr. Phillimore, that Sergeant Crouch asked you* (on 4th March) *whether you had seen Pike on the road to Enford?*" asked the barrister.

"*The sergeant did not, but Superintendent Buchanan did the next day.*"

"*How would he know to ask? He had not seen Pike in the meantime.*"

"*I told him I had not seen Pike in the house, but I did not say anything about having passed him on the road.*"

"*So you made a mistake just now?*" said Parr, with mock politeness.

Walter did not answer, and that was that. The apparent overturning of the *alibi* evidence became the hinge on which the matter now swung, even though Ernest's case should have been considered quite strong enough to refute Crouch's skimpy evidence without it. The very fact that the most powerful evidence now appeared to be untrue cast doubt on Pike's whole version of events, an impression strongly reinforced by young Tom Phillimore's failure to turn up at the Inquiry. A society which was always ready to accept that the ends justified the means where police investigations were concerned accepted that if the Chief Constable's suspicions were right then his methods were too.

Emma Phillimore was called, and was again very emphatic that Ernest had not been in the pub, but Phillimore believability had been compromised by the apparent breaking of the Chisenbury *alibi* and by Tom's absence. His evidence was undoubtedly important, but his parent's explanation was that he was needed in Enford to mind the business, an excuse which now seemed limp given the way the father's evidence had been overturned.[61]

You can't help wondering though

Immaterial it may be in the grand scheme, but it is impossible not to be intrigued by the question of what really happened at Enford on the 4th March, so what are we to make of Walter Phillimore's apparent *volte face* concerning seeing Ernest Pike on the road. Had this really given the *coup de grace* to any thought of Ernest's innocence? Certainly it was extremely damaging, but having been critical of Llewellyn's claim to have decided the case upon one man's demeanour before an inquiry, it behoves us to take care not to do the same, and on reflection a straightforward explanation becomes apparent.

Parr suggested that Buchanan could not have known to <u>ask</u> about the *alibi* on the morning of 5th March when he called Phillimore to see him. But Pike, according to his own report, told Crouch about it on the Monday night, and if this is so, then Buchanan is certain to have been apprised of it the following morning. Now this requires us to believe this particular point in Pike's account written a week after the incident. Why should we?

There are two reasons:

First, we know Buchanan took every opportunity to attempt to cast doubt on any evidence favouring Pike, going to ludicrous lengths to discredit him, yet he never denied this aspect of Pike's report. All he managed to say in his letter which covered the report was that an

---

[61] The author has seen later (1950s) evidence which states that Tom was of limited ability. This probably explains the reason why he was not called as a witness.

accompanying statement by Tom Phillimore had been penned in Ernest Pike's hand (which was normal, as long as the signature is authentic, and we might surmise was particularly necessary if Tom would have difficulty in composing and writing his own statement).

Second, the Buchanans and Llewellyn declared to the Inquiry that all statements and reports had been gone through with the utmost thoroughness. Whether or not they believed in the truth of the *alibi*, they never cast doubt on what Pike said that he told Crouch. So if it follows that the Buchanans and Llewellyn accepted that Pike made the claim of the *alibi* to Crouch on the night of the 4th March, the grounds upon which Parr refuted it therefore don't hold water.

So why didn't Phillimore stick to his guns? If he had intended to lie, he could have said that he volunteered the information to Buchanan without being asked – that would have been credible enough. But he may have been genuinely puzzled by the apparent discrepancy that Parr sprang upon him in the witness box. Walter would not have known what Crouch had already said to Buchanan by the time the superintendent questioned the publican on 5th March.

Inexperienced witnesses sometimes mentally panic when faced with a conundrum. If they cannot think fast enough to give a rational explanation, a clever lawyer can quickly terminate the examination with great advantage. English legal procedures recognise the danger, and allow re-examination by the friendly advocate which can re-establish the proper context, but Smith didn't exercise this right. Perhaps he might have been unsure of how his witness would perform if it came to a direct clash of evidence with the police, for no publican liked to fall foul of the local constabulary, especially of a superintendent with a patent capacity for long-term grudge carrying. By standing his ground Walter would have been quite justified in fearing for his licence when it came up for renewal at the Brewster Sessions, for the police would have no difficulty in producing an objection which the magistrates would act upon.[62]

---

[62] The danger of running foul of the police was a real one for publicans. At the April 1901 S.J.C. meeting, the Chairman Sir Godfrey Lushington had opined that as Wiltshire was a rural county with very little crime, then the *most important* job of the police was to

They Doth Protest Too Much

The desire of the Pikes and Hanks to show that there was a strain of family insanity was motivated by the desire to see the inquest verdict ameliorated for Amelia's financial benefit, and to lessen any stain on the family reputation.

The claims in the Hanks/Morse letter, now repeated by another relative in the box, William Ponting of Malmesbury, were consequently over enthusiastic. Although great strides were then being made in the understanding and sympathetic treatment of mental disorders, there was much misdiagnosis by today's standards and 'insanity' was the pronouncement upon many forms of inexplicable or antisocial behaviour. Symptoms of physical illnesses were often represented as insanity, and the disorder from which Pike's mother Susannah was said to have suffered, 'puerperal insanity', is today understood as post-natal depression, an unpleasant condition which can cause grossly uncharacteristic behaviour, but not something which would be inherited, at least by male progeny. This is not to suggest that Ernest should not have been entitled to an inquest verdict of temporary insanity though, for such uncharacteristic behaviour brought on by overwhelming stress was routinely referred to as temporary insanity.

Keating Comes Good Eventually

As Mr Ponting finished giving his evidence about mental instability, William Keating added unhelpfully that he knew Ernest was excitable, which, coming from him seems to be a bit rich. With incredible

---

control the public houses! The police were not sympathetic to publicans, as a case in Swindon in January 1898 shows. Stanley Soper, landlord of the Bell and Shoulder of Mutton was falsely accused of an offence by a drunken, aggrieved policeman. Robinson and Sterne pressed the charge, which would have resulted in the loss of Soper's licence. Fortunately, in this case the magistrate stopped the case on hearing the defence evidence, much to the displeasure of Sterne.

The consumption of intoxicating liquor was not a prerequisite for a prosecution of policemen improperly in licensed premises, or for the landlord accused of harbouring them. In April 1913, publican James Penman of Hamilton was convicted of harbouring two constables in his public house contrary to the Licensing Act (Scotland) 1903 s62 (1), the relevant provisions of which were identical to the English Licensing Consolidation Act. The men in blue had not taken a drink, but had merely eaten oat cake and sardines as sustenance during a long period on duty.

insensitivity given the nature of the two policemen's deaths, he added that when he and Ernest had been out shooting together he often felt frightened to stay.

The Chairman politely asked the reverend gentleman whether he would now like to give evidence. Keating said no thank you; he did not think he would unless it was absolutely necessary! One wonders what he thought he was there for, and so presumably did Radcliffe who very tactfully guided him, "*Well, it is entirely a matter for you, if you think you can throw any light on the case*".

Keating changed his mind, abandoned the lawyers table and entered the box. If he was there to represent Ernest Pike's dying wishes, he was equally keen to justify himself, and admitted as much to the assembled multitude before launching in to an explanation of his relationship with the Chief Constable. Mr Radcliffe courteously asked him to come to something nearer to the point, but the elderly vicar carried on with little alteration in his content or style. He said that he had "*never presumed to interfere* (in police matters) *as he was too much of a gentleman, and had too much common sense.*" Llewellyn must have bitten deep into his lip when he heard this.

Keating churned over well furrowed ground in his explanation of his own feelings about the case, without adding anything startlingly new, and revealed the 'cannot separate us' conversation he had with Ernest on 6th March.

"*Separate who?*" asked Radcliffe.

Keating explained for him.

Keating was now asked for, but declined to give, the identity of his source of information about the spurious cases involving other policemen which he had raised, an act which pointedly indicated his distrust of the police and S.J.C. hierarchy, and for which he was praised in the *Police Review* report of the inquiry. Radcliffe's motives in asking the question seem to have been an attempt on behalf of the Chief Constable to find out who the troublemakers in the force were.

Returning to the subject of Ernest Pike, Keating now slowly worked himself up. In reply to a question from Radcliffe with regard to Ernest's state of mind, he said:

"I never noticed anything wrong with his mind; he was always clear, though when excited his eyes used to shoot out of his head. He was a most keen officer, and I never saw a keener man. He never neglected his duty, and he was not a man addicted to drink. He only drank like myself or the Chief Constable, and to say that he was addicted to drink was false[63]*. My only reason for coming forward was that he wrote that letter to me, and I thought it my duty to vindicate his character, so that it might be proved to the world that he was not a murderer and that he did this because he was under a sense of insanity, and that he was not fairly judged or tried."*

This passionate statement was well received in many parts of the courtroom, and applause broke out to the consternation of the Chairman who angrily threatened to expel the public if there was any more. He reprimanded Keating for making a florid address, to which the vicar replied,

"Have I said enough?"

"No," said Radcliffe.

"Nothing more than I desire to say..." said Keating

Mr Parr spoke up, and another bad tempered exchange took place.

Parr: *"Do you still suggest that Pike was not allowed to defend himself?"*

Keating: *"I don't believe he was. I am not satisfied. He had no witness brought forward."*

Parr: *"Had you any knowledge (of this) at all when you wrote to the papers?"*

Keating: *"I had his letters."*

Parr: *"Do you put yourself forward as a gentleman who in this matter has a high sense of justice yourself?"*

---

[63] Those of his children old enough to remember their father would say in later years that they never saw him the worse for drink.

Keating: "*Has that anything to do with the matter?*"

Parr: "*I want to know! If you have a high sense of justice, don't you think it would have been better to have asked the Chief Constable as to whether Pike was allowed to defend himself or bring witnesses?*"

Keating: "*You forget that the Chief Constable failed to answer my letter to him.*"

Parr sat down. Keating exploded.

"*This inquiry*", he yelled, "*is the last straw!*"

He was wrong again. Further burdens would be heaped upon the Pike family.

Who Better to Have the Last Word?

Mrs Pike, who had been sitting with her family in the petty jury box indicated that she wished to say something else in addition to her earlier evidence, and she was invited to do so now by Mr Radcliffe. She did not take to the witness box, but simply stood up and addressed the assemblage:

"*My husband came home and said to me: the Chief Constable took no notice of statements. The Chief Constable said, 'As for statements, I take no notice of them; I thoroughly believe that you were in that house.' That is what my husband came home and told me that same night.*"

Radcliffe asked her:

"*Did he say the Chief Constable said he took no notice of statements by people in licensed houses?*"

"*No, sir; he said, 'As for statements, I take no notice of them. I thoroughly believe you were in that house.'*"

Llewellyn was not called upon to answer this statement, and the inquiry had now reached its end, after some 6 hours. It was not a trial, so there was no climax of a verdict to be reached by a jury or magistrates; the evidence would, in theory at any rate, be sifted and weighed by the three commissioners of the sub-committee, who would in due course report their findings to a full session of the Wiltshire Standing Joint Committee. Mr Parr pointed out that their next scheduled meeting was not due to take place for some time and in view of the public interest that the case had aroused he hoped that there might be arrangements made to speed things up. Sir John Goldney responded encouragingly that indeed there might be.

Keating Sees Where He Might Have Gone Wrong

The horse drawn drive home from Devizes Assize Courts to the Vicarage at Wilsford took about 45 minutes, and so by about 5.30 p.m. the Reverend W.W. Keating was probably back in the familiar surroundings of the home where he had lived since 1881. There was tea to have, maybe a fortifying sherry after the events of the day – after all, this was a country vicarage – and essential duties and prayers to attend to, but when he had time to reflect he must have been embarrassed by his public performance, for next morning the vicar's overworked pen was again in action as he wrote to the editor of the *Wiltshire Gazette*.

DEAR MR EDITOR.

I beg to state that I was far too overwrought when I entered the witness box yesterday afternoon to say all I meant to say. I did not realise till the last moment that I would be allowed to enter the witness-box to give evidence or I should have been better prepared to do so. I now wish to say that if, in my over zeal to carry out P.C. Pike's wishes in his letter to me of March 31st, as well as my desire to speak in the name of the public as requested, and to benefit the force in general, I have in my letter to Mr Medlicott and the Wiltshire Gazette of April 10th overdone the mark, and used unguarded language, I am quite willing to acknowledge it, and I regret it if I have done so. I must say in vindication of myself that if the Chief Constable was, as he evidently appeared to be, annoyed by my approaching him concerning P.C. Pike, either by interview or letter, three times in four years, it would have been fairer on his part both to me and the late P.C. Pike to have written and told me so, as then I should not have approached him anymore. Also, as to my visits to Pike and his family, if I was, as the Chief Constable insinuated at Amesbury on April (sic) 31st to P.C. Pike, injuring Pike in any way by these visits it would have been fairer of the Chief Constable to *have acquainted me or Pike of this fact months ago, and then I should have ceased to visit the Pikes, as considering my friendship with them, I should have been the last who would desire in any way to injure them. As to the tittle-tattle talk, which was mentioned by Mr Parr, in connection with these visits (which always took place on the childrens' birthdays)*, if it existed at Enford Pike would have been the very first to hear it and to tell me about it (also Mr Branfoot, the Vicar, who is a friend of mine, and knew of these visits as well), and Pike would have requested me not to visit them anymore. The strange part is that I was in the habit of visiting Pike at intervals for three years and nine months and nothing was said about it until Supt. Buchanan came into this division.*

I beg to say that as regards Pike's state of mind on the night of March 31st, no stronger point could be produced than the fact that by committing this crime he forgot completely his wife and family, and the injury it would bring upon them. Now Pike was a first-rate husband and a good and affectionate father.

I trust, and the public do also, that the Standing Joint Committee will see their way to give a pension to Mrs Pike, who has been dependent on her good husband and left a widow with six helpless children.

May 9th 1913   I remain, yours faithfully, W. W. KEATING

*(Keating missed 31st March, the day of the Amesbury hearing and George Pike's second birthday).

The press reported the whole inquiry in detail, but uncritically. It was left to the *Police Review* to provide editorial comment in an article which one senses was written with an effort of self-control:

"The Inquiry has been held, and it was certainly a full one, in a sense, going into numerous extraneous details, and including more or less gushing statements by counsel, not strictly bearing upon the main question of the proof of Pike's guilt and the justice of his punishment. The Investigating Committee was not constituted as we should have advised in a case of such importance. We say this without reference to their decision, and without taking the slightest exception to their procedure. We write this article in advance of the Report, and without the slightest suspicion as to what their conclusions may be, although we have refrained from publishing our own views until their Report has appeared. But

we do think it would have been more advisable to submit the whole case to a Commission appointed by the Home Secretary: entirely removed from local associations or influences; and we think it better to say this in advance, and with no motive that might be imputed to any difference that may be found to exist between the Committee's conclusions and our own."[64]

This need for an independent Home Office Inquiry was clear to any reasonable observer; the good folk of Enford had expected it, the Police Review advised it, and there would be yet more calls for it before long.

The cost of the Inquiry was born by the County. It amounted to £61 15s 6d.

---

[64] *'Police Review and Parade Gossip'*, 20th June 1913. This was written before the Inquiry Report had been made public, but printed afterwards.

Chapter 9

Drawing Breath

A five week hiatus now occurred, whilst the county waited for the next act in the unfolding drama. Newspapers made no comment about the case apart from short reports about the progress of an appeal fund set up for Mrs Pike by Keating which seems to have attracted generous contributions within Wiltshire and the surrounding counties, though a similar national fund set up by Kempster of the *Police Review* was disappointingly supported.

Whilst we are waiting for the Inquiry Report to come in, this is a good point for us to take advantage of the respite to look a little further into some aspects of contemporary practice in the conduct of inquests, for much will subsequently be said on the subject.

- There was no specific rule concerning the timing of an inquest after death had been reported to the coroner, so long as bodies were not allowed to putrefy,[64] though what guidelines existed were all concerned with preventing delay by a coroner. No one had thought that excessive haste might ever be a problem.

    Sylvester had a reputation for being quick, and there are some other instances of him holding suicide inquests on the same day as bodies were discovered. In September 1913 he inquired into the case of Walter King of Devizes on the same day as the body was discovered. Here though, there were no contentious details, the circumstances were clear and the coroner's travelling time to Devizes was well under half that of the journey to Coombe. Nevertheless, proceedings did not commence until 4.00 p.m., 10½ hours after the discovery of the body had been reported. Pike's case remains his record by a long way.

- Judges, Coroners and magistrates have long been protected against any form of action for anything which they do in court in pursuance

---

[64] re Hull, 1882.

of their official functions, a principle repeated by Lord Chief Justice Tenterden in 1827,[65] although four decades later it was made clear that this protection was simply to ensure that judges could exercise their duties without fear of consequences, not to protect the malicious or corrupt.[66]

- Certain parties had a right to examine witnesses, including family and any personal representatives of the deceased, but there was no duty upon the coroner to advise these people of the arrangements for inquest, nor that they had the right to examine, and to be legally represented.

- The Coroners standard text book [67] specified that inquests should not be held at any hour that might cause inconvenience to any who have to attend. Sylvester must surely have known that relatives from outside the immediate area might wish to come to the inquest and possibly bring some evidence. By holding the inquest so quickly it could certainly be argued that he constructively prevented their attendance and contravened this guideline. However, there was no legal obligation upon a coroner to inform even the nearest relatives of the arrangements for, or result of, an inquest.

- It was for coroners to determine who would be called before their courts, but where they refused to hear potential witnesses who were available to give evidence, or where they declined to call such witnesses *and as a result made insufficient inquiry*, the verdict could be quashed.[68]

Apart from preventing relatives attending, the timing of the Coombe inquest also meant that the suicide notes had not come to light. Of course nobody knew for certain that Pike had written any until they appeared out of the postal system, but the coroner would know that such missives were very common in this sort of case and

---

[65] Garnett v Farrand.
[66] Scott v Stansfield, 1868.
[67] Jervis: Offices and Duties of Coroners, 1898 edition.
[68] CR v Carter, 1876.

so there was a strong likelihood that one or more might exist. Nobody asked Amelia Pike before or during the inquest whether she had knowledge of any.

Sylvester himself said that the evidence regarding Crouch's shooting by Pike was circumstantial, so any potential doubt might have been lifted by an adjournment which allowed notes or other evidence to come to light. If he and Llewellyn suspected that Pike had put pen to paper though, they would know that the contents of any notes would be certain to be embarrassing for the police and for Llewellyn. It is hard to escape the conclusion that the extreme rapidity with which the inquest was held, and which Llewellyn said "*suited my convenience*" was a deliberate ploy to finalise matters before any embarrassing truths came into the open. At that point of course nobody knew that Keating was ready to raise the roof, and it would have been thought that a rapid inquest would wrap up a potentially embarrassing business.

Other Places, Other Cases

Sylvester was often generous in accepting insanity as a suicidal factor and he was sometimes excessively keen for his jurymen to find it, as in the case of an army officer faced with a financial scandal who shot himself at Devizes only two weeks before Pike's suicide at Coombe.[69] He sometimes went to great lengths to prevent *felo de se* verdicts. His jury direction at his inquest into the death of Percy Bird of Melksham on 2nd July 1914 provides an interesting comparison to what he said to Foreman Tilley at Coombe. Sylvester now told his jury that the 'customary' verdict allowing unsound mind was sometimes a mistake, as some evidence of imbalance was needed.

There was no such evidence in Bird's case, but, said the coroner, *this still did not mean that their verdict should necessarily be felo de se*. They could say that their finding was 'suicide with insufficient evidence of state of mind'. In reading Sylvester's jury directions for various cases,

---

[69] The case of Lt (Quartermaster) G H Martin, 1st Bn Wiltshire Regiment, who was sent to the Devizes depôt from Gibraltar to give evidence in connection with a canteen funds scandal.

one is left with a distinct impression that he thought of the *felo de se* verdict as a punishment, to be handed down upon those of whose actions he disapproved. One of his earlier firearm murder/suicide inquiries is indicative of this.

The Holt Tragedy, April 1908

In 1908 the west Wiltshire village of Holt was the home of Mrs Rebecca Meaden. She was the wife of Fred Meaden, a soldier who had spent many years in India, and it seems that she eased her loneliness by associating with another soldier, Charles Vinall, who was stationed at Portsmouth. Husband Fred's time in the ranks was up in 1908, and he returned to Holt to resume married life, but the fireworks which might have been expected when he found out about Vinall were not forthcoming, as he seemed tolerant of his wife's faithlessness.

Nevertheless, a tense situation arose when Vinall realised that his association with Rebecca was now over. On Saturday, 4th April he travelled to Holt carrying a revolver which he had purchased in Portsmouth. At about 1.30 p.m. he shot Rebecca dead in the kitchen of her cottage, and then shot himself through the mouth, falling dead across the body of his victim.

Sylvester conducted the inquest at Holt the following Monday morning. The facts were straightforward. Sylvester made it clear that he was particularly keen that *felo de se* should be the verdict on Vinall, not because he had any sort of evidence as to the soundness of Vinall's mind, but because of what he clearly felt was the despicable crime of shooting a woman. Despite his clear personal feelings in the matter though, and his advice to the jury to return a verdict of *felo de se*, Sylvester did his duty at Holt properly (in clear contrast to his behaviour at Pike's inquest), and specifically raised the question of the possible mental state of the killer, making it clear in his summing up to the jury that they had a duty to consider it, and a right to temper their verdict accordingly.

Having been properly informed of their responsibilities, the Holt jury concurred with Sylvester's wishes, and decided that Vinall had been sane, and had thus committed the 'felony of himself'.

Dangerous Durham

Remarkable as it may seem, Colonel White, a nineteenth century Chief Constable of County Durham, was faced with two incidents involving the murder of officers by ex-policemen, followed by the suicides of the assailants.

In April 1868, 31 year old P.C. John Cruikshank of Pittington laid a complaint against another constable, David Paton of Sherburn, alleging drunkenness. The matter was investigated by White on 1st May and Paton was acquitted. Cruikshank then went on to point out that Paton had previously been dismissed from a Scottish force and had not declared this when he joined the Durham Constabulary, and faced with this true information White had no option but to dismiss Paton from the force. After the hearing Paton shot Cruikshank with a revolver in a determined attack in which after wounding his victim with two shots he pursued Cruikshank into a public house where he fired a third and fatal shot into the injured man's chest. He then walked outside and shot himself in the head, falling into the arms of a third policeman named MacKay. The inquest on both men was held next day in the public house where Cruikshank's body still lay, the Lambton Arms in Sherburn, and a verdict of wilful murder by Paton was passed.

The second incident occurred in Silver Street, Durham twenty years later in bizarre circumstances. On 31st May 1888 a superintendent named Scott had arrived in the city from Jarrow by train in order to collect his mens' wages and also to deliver a prisoner, a man named Fannen, to the County Gaol. On leaving the railway station the pair were approached from behind by a man who pulled a rifle from a gun case and shot the superintendent in the back, causing him to collapse immediately, still handcuffed to the presumably incredulous Fannen. Dropping the rifle, the assailant then produced a pistol with which he shot himself through the mouth, dying instantly. Scott died shortly afterwards without regaining consciousness. The killer, Benjamin Wright, had served as a sergeant under Scott until the previous August, when he had been reduced in rank and posted to Darlington for disciplinary offences. Whilst there he committed further offences for which he was dismissed from the force.

The inquest was held the same day, and found that Scott had been wilfully murdered by Wright.

In neither of these two cases was a verdict of *felo de se* passed on the suicides: in Paton's case coroner Mr Crofton Maynard declared that '*as to his own* (Paton's) *death, a verdict of suicide, but whether in a sane or insane state of mind there was not sufficient evidence to show*'. Wright was found to be temporarily insane. Of course, in neither case were the murder victims killed by a serving officer, even though Paton had only been dismissed earlier the same day. The Coombe case of one serving police officer murdering another and then committing suicide remains horribly unique in mainland Britain.[70]

The One Before .....

In the space of the six months bracketing the Coombe deaths, three other policemen in England had met death by shooting. On 9th October 1912 Inspector Arthur Walls of the Eastbourne Police was shot and killed whilst responding to a report of burglary. The killer, George Mackay (also known as John Williams) was arrested a little over a month later, and was hanged at Lewes Prison on 29th January 1913.

..... and the Two After.

A fortnight after the bodies of Frank Crouch and Ernest Pike had been discovered, John Amos, tenant of the Sun Inn in Bedlington in Northumberland, found himself being evicted by the freeholder of his business. After giving immediate notice to quit to Amos, the owner and licensee John Wood Irons, returned to the inn with new tenants, Richard and Sarah Grice, plus a couple of his employees to assist with

---

[70] Four nineteenth century cases in the Royal Irish Constabulary and one in the Royal Ulster Constabulary in 1940 can not be directly compared.

the stock check. In view of Amos's aggressive attitude he had thought it prudent to ask the local bobby, P.C. George Mussell to accompany them.

The main part of the group descended to the cellar, leaving Sarah and George in the bar; Amos almost immediately pulled out a rifle which he kept behind the bar and shot Sarah in the head, upon which, fatally injured, she fell down the cellar stairs. He now pointed the rifle at George who bravely kept Amos talking whilst the remainder of the party managed to make good their escape from the cellar. As they ran another shot rang out, and George fell dead. A commotion had now arisen outside the pub, and another policeman was soon on the scene. In an act of the most astonishing bravery, knowing that Amos had probably already killed twice and had nothing to lose, Sergeant Andrew Barton walked calmly across the deserted open ground in front of the pub, and in through the door to do his duty and effect an arrest. He was immediately shot dead.

Amos came to the door, put down his rifle, and smoking a cigarette he called out that he wanted Irons to show himself, so that he could shoot him too. With the arrival of more policemen, one of them an Inspector armed with a revolver, Amos took flight. He sought refuge in a drainage culvert, and a local man named Potter offered to help the police. Potter owned a rifle, and he was instructed to fire into the culvert, his shots hitting Amos in the head causing a superficial wound. Amos now surrendered, and after trial at Newcastle this triple murderer was hanged at the prison there on 22nd July 1913.

Chapter 10

Last Chance for Justice

The Inquiry Report is submitted
Trowbridge, Wednesday 11th June 1913

A little over a month after the Devizes Inquiry seventeen members of the Standing Joint Committee met in extraordinary session in Trowbridge to accept the official report. Fourteen were magistrates some of them double-hatted with council seats as well, an earl, a marquis, three knights, an Admiral and two Kings Counsels amongst them. Only three were there by sole virtue of holding a county council seat.

The report had been principally authored by Radcliffe K.C. At the opening of the Inquiry, it will be remembered, he had said that the Enford Parish Council complaints were the basis of the investigation, and that Keating's allegations were a "side issue which they could not keep off". He now told the Committee that the matters which the sub-committee had been asked to investigate were complaints made by Keating in his 9th April letter to Medlicott. This unexplained alteration of emphasis with a 'side issue' now being presented as the central contention is typical of the inconsistencies which occurred time and again in the official handling of events. The sub-committee had condensed the contents of that letter to the following seven point format:

1. That P.C. Pike was unfairly dealt with at the Amesbury inquiry by the Chief Constable, and that justice was not done to him; that he was not allowed to defend himself, or produce the statements of his witnesses.

2. Inferentially, that P.C. Pike was in fact innocent of the matters charged against him.

3. That this was the fourth case, to Mr Keating's knowledge, in which the Chief Constable has acted in a similar manner.

4. That the Chief Constable should not be allowed absolute power in cases.
5. That the inquest was conducted with unseemly haste, and that no evidence was submitted to the jury as to P.C. Pike's state of mind.
6. That in fact P.C. Pike was insane.
7. That the Chief Constable had falsely accused Mr Keating of immoral relations with P.C. Pike's wife.

The vagueness of stated aims prior to the inquiry, and the obvious intention of the sub-committee to limit areas of discussion are obvious from the preamble to the report. Radcliffe's words, but my emphases:

"*Having regard to the fact that the terms of the reference to us **were somewhat uncertain**, and the inquiry itself **more or less of an informal character**, we first considered **amongst ourselves** which of the above – mentioned subjects were matters which we could deal with as delegates of the Standing Joint Committee. We came to the conclusion that as regards question No.4 in as much as the Chief Constable's position is statutory, under provisions which apply to every Police Force in the country, no useful object would be gained by an inquiry on our part into the policy of Parliament in the matter. And, as regards question No.5, inasmuch as the Standing Joint Committee has no authority over the Coroner, we considered it beyond our powers to conduct any inquiry into his conduct. While saying this, we do not for a moment suggest that his conduct was otherwise than strictly correct and in accordance with law.*"

The first and second points in the list should have been treated separately and distinctly, for Pike's innocence or otherwise of the Three Horse Shoes affair should not have obscured the question of whether he had been fairly treated over it. But the almost universal acceptance of ends justifying means prevailed once again.

Llewellyn Exonerated

As to the conduct of the Amesbury hearing, the sub-committee only had the evidence of the Chief Constable and the two Buchanans to go by, which they unreservedly accepted, repeating Llewellyn's assertion that Crouch had given an impressive performance whilst Pike harmed himself by his poor demeanour. There was no bias, said the report, in the minds of any of the policemen accusing Pike. There was no reference to Archibald Buchanan's notes to Llewellyn, the tone of which convincingly show this statement to be completely untrue.

Whatever the truth of the Three Horse Shoes affair, Crouch they said, was personally convinced that his own version was correct. This was a spectacularly clever conclusion for them to draw, given that they had never had the opportunity to question him on the matter! Here, we may observe, is a slight move towards acceptance that Crouch may have been wrong.

They decided that P.C. Pike had every opportunity to defend himself against Crouch's charge. They made great play of Tom Phillimore's failure to attend the inquiry and his father's apparent change of heart concerning the Chisenbury *alibi*. These points were certainly damaging to the Pike faction, but as we have seen there are sound explanations. The three lawyers who formed the sub-committee of inquiry, should have seen through the flimsy grounds on which they were based, and even if solicitor Smith had not been particularly effective in refuting them, they had a duty to draw balanced conclusions in their report. Instead, they played along with the game of ensuring that no blame attached itself to any member of the establishment. That left only one primary defence witness to dispose of:

"The evidence of Walter Phillimore's wife who was called before us, did not impress us favourably," they wrote, (without giving any explanation whatsoever as to why this conclusion was reached), thus neatly squaring away all the direct evidence.

'*Upon a review of the whole of the facts we have come to a clear opinion that the decision of the Chief Constable was right. It is at least certain that he came to an honest conclusion upon facts which fairly warranted it.*' The certainty in the first sentence of this comment is immediately qualified by an acceptance of the possibility of mistake in the second.

Keating Shown Up Again

The report dealt with point number 3, the red herrings raised by Keating, at unnecessary length, even though these had no bearing whatsoever on the case and no attempt was made to investigate them properly. The overall effect was to discredit Keating's credibility and imply a sense of personal maliciousness against the Chief Constable.

New Laws Made to Order

With hindsight we can see that the question of Pike's sanity was one which the Standing Joint Committee was ready to allow after their 24th April 'way forward' meeting when they withdrew from public session. Of course they may have genuinely felt the inquest verdict to be too harsh, but it can be seen that they now knew that the benefit of advantage lay with accepting that Pike was unbalanced at the end, for:

- An acceptance of insanity would go some way to satisfying the family, Keating and others, deterring further agitation which might have led to an independent inquiry.

- A suggestion of insanity would, by Llewellyn's logic, 'lessen the slur on the Force'.

- Llewellyn's abominable reflection on Amelia's good name would have been considered too much by all levels of society. No gentleman would say such a thing about an obviously respectable woman. Pike held that Llewellyn *had* said it though; according to his suicide notes, it was the thing which tipped him over the edge.[72]

---

[72] Llewellyn's attitude towards women was always aggressive. Twice married to divorcées, but childless, he imposed rules upon his force by banning married men from acknowledging their wives whilst in uniform. He issued instructions that women were to be banned from polling stations in the 1910 General Election. He required constables who wished to marry to produce references for their fiancées, and even instituted restrictive rules on women with who constables under training might consort. He stood in the way of constable's wives who wished to work, and strongly resisted the introduction of WPCs.

The Chief Constable denied making it of course, but this was unconvincing if Pike were 'sane', for why should a man in possession of his mental faculties come to such a conclusion with so much certainty that he would take his own life? The only way to explain it and get Llewellyn's reputation off the hook was to declare Pike to have been mad.

However the sub-committee had no power to alter the inquest verdict. They could not criticise the coroner who had only done his bit to help Llewellyn, for this would risk alerting authorities who had the power to lift the inquest into the High Court by certiorari. So somehow the sub-committee had to declare Pike insane, the coroner and the verdict right, and Llewellyn blameless. Quite a dilemma, but fear naught, they were up to the challenge. Totally without legal authority or benefit of medical advice they introduced a new category of insanity.

"We are convinced that though he may not have been 'insane' in the legal sense, Pike was deranged in mind at the time when he took Sergeant Crouch's life and his own," they wrote, going on to say that *"We have no doubt that on the night of 31st March his mind was completely off its balance."*

The inability to control ones emotions under great stress leading to suicide nearly always resulted in a temporary insanity verdicts, and if this is what the sub-committee felt to have been the case on the night of 31st March they should have said so, and recommended a review of the coroner's finding. Such a procedure would inevitably have cast light on the actions of the coroner and Chief Constable though, and they instead indulged in this contradictory claptrap.[73]

In closing their report, the commissioners opined that, insofar as the consideration of an award of a gratuity to Mrs Pike was concerned, then what had happened might be seen as a terrible misfortune rather than a great crime, and they drew attention to Pike's years of good

---

[73] The refusal to overtly criticise an official (in this case Sylvester) whilst simultaneously debunking what he has done finds a parallel in the 1924 Judicial inquiry, where all of John Syme's complaints were agreed to be well founded, yet no criticism of senior policemen's actions was made. (See page 15).

service, repeating their opinion that he had been deranged on March 31st. The dead constable's family had succeeded, they said, in removing a considerable stigma from his name. If this was indeed so, the committee should have initiated steps to bring the matter before the High Court, for the Pikes should have had a right to see the quashing of the inquest verdict. But of course, nothing of the kind was suggested, and the Pikes were expected to be content with the Standing Joint Committee's not-so-gracious nod in their direction.

The report recommended that the legal costs of the Chief Constable and also of the Pike family be met from county funds, and in one further oblique inference to their acceptance of temporary derangement, they recommended that inquiry should be made into the existence of hereditary insanity in the family of any man applying to join the police.

Back Slapping

Radcliffe, Medlicott and Goldney placed their signatures to this appalling document and commended it to the Standing Joint Committee which commented upon it as "wise and thorough". But the matter was not going to lie down and go away just yet. Any appearance of acquiescence amongst the seventeen men in the chamber was an illusion.

Somebody Speaks Up

The sub-committee's report recommended payment of a gratuity to Amelia, and the accounts committee (not an independent body, but simply one comprised of some members of the S.J.C. including Radnor and Goldney) had put their minds to the matter. The maximum which might legally be allowed was £100, but the sum recommended by the Accounts Committee was £52. This was a truly paltry total, just two thirds of Ernest's annual salary of £76 10s, and it would not even be paid at once and in full, but was to be granted at the rate ten shillings (50 pence) a week for two years. It was good enough for Mr G.A.R. Fitzgerald K.C. and Sir Richard Pollen though, and they moved and seconded the recommendation.

At last, at long, long last, somebody in a position of authority finally spoke up. Reuben George, man of the people, showed the decency which had been absent from the official handling of this whole sorry business right from its start. He was the new boy on the Joint Committee, an elected County Councillor rather than one of the powerful gentlemen from the County Magistrates Bench, and the reason why he had not spoken earlier was to become a little clearer before the day was out.

Mr George's point now was that £52 was miserly and if the subcommittee's findings of mental instability at the time of death were accepted as having credence, then there was no reason to treat Ernest's family other than generously, for he had simply been a sick unfortunate at the time of his death. In this he was supported by the Reverend Henry Bagley Bardwell, who comes across the years as a well-meaning and kind spirited man, but one who had a rather vague grasp of the powers and limitations of the committee, showing a propensity for asking vacuous questions. Bardwell was a Baptist who ran a school in Chippenham, and his fellow nonconformist Reuben George would be glad of his support, for Reuben's was otherwise a lone voice, much like that of Walker who had stood alone for justice against his fellow S.J.C. members in 1901.

The hatchet-faced Fitzgerald K.C., who had leapt to propose accepting the £52 recommendation (his own recommendation as he was on the accounts committee), now demonstrated the mood of the majority of the S.J.C. He reminded the meeting that the award of *any* sum at all was a matter of grace. There was a public collection taking place for Mrs Pike, said Fitzgerald, which should be taken into account, and anyway, places in the police orphanage had been arranged as a means of relieving the financial strain on the young family. Well, that was all right then! If the awful position that children of a police killer would find themselves in at the Police Orphanage occurred to Fitzgerald and the others like him, it does not seem to have concerned them.

Readers will form their own opinion of Mr Gerald Augustus Robert Fitzgerald, King's Counsel, from the record of his words to which I need add nothing, but Lord Radnor could see no fault with the elderly barrister's views. The noble Earl added that far from being miserly it was a moot point whether any gratuity should be awarded at all, given the circumstances. He thought that an award of *any* size would be very generous, (*"Hear, Hear !!"*) rang from this assemblage of wealthy men at this expression of aristocratic compassion toward a widow with six young children).

Recommendation of the amount having thus been accepted, approval was needed for the disbursement of the paltry sum. The Marquis of Bath was graciously pleased to propose, it was seconded by Admiral Wilson, and the proposal was carried.[74]

Go for it, Reuben ....

A vote of thanks to the investigating sub-committee was now proposed, a sure sign that proceedings were coming to an end. Reuben George started to rumble. He had been tricked — he had things to say, he was waiting patiently and courteously for the right point in the proceedings, and now it was being wrapped up before he had said his piece. In his long association with various county committees he knew that it was normal for a clause by clause debate to follow formal acceptance of reports. That was what he was waiting for, and why he had not so far spoken up. He mentioned to Radnor that he would like normal procedures followed. Earl Radnor's reply was not at all what he thought he would hear; there would be no opportunity to discuss the report in this way. *"Quite out of the question"*, said the noble Lord.

George was able to start speaking by taking the opportunity to pay lip service to the vote of thanks, but instead of stopping after the routine obsequies he kept right on going with an attack on Llewellyn.

"Why", said George, *"did the Chief Constable not call witnesses at the Amesbury hearing, which, I gather lasted for about half-an-......."*

---

[74] The sum was finally reported as having been fully paid at the S.J.C. meeting on 8th July 1915, by which time it had been necessary to add the sum of eighteen shillings and seven pence (92½p) in interest for deferred instalments.

He was not allowed to finish his question.

Radnor: *"I don't think we can hold a court of inquiry here, Mr George. That would be quite out of the question."*

Reuben George: *"I quite feel that, my lord. I don't want in any way to feel unfriendly towards the Chief Constable, but feel this – that it would be the best opportunity for clearing the air with regard to this matter. They feel opportunities were not given at the time."*

Radnor: *"I am afraid we cannot allow this. I am very sorry, but with the best will in the world, if you or any member of the Committee are going to interfere with the discretion of the Chief Constable in matters of discipline, I can assure you we could not do our work efficiently, and I am certain the county could not be served as it is."*

(In this remark by the Earl we seem to be close to the truth. Nobody, not even the Committee which was the regulating body for the County Police, was to be allowed to 'interfere' with the Chief Constable's disciplinary procedures, the 'One Man System'. The excuse that had been given at the Devizes Inquiry for refusing to look at this was that a Parliamentary review was underway. Radnor had now made it clear that the real reason was that the Standing Joint Committee – most of them anyway – did not want change).

Reuben George was not finished yet:

"Well, I must say I don't feel satisfied", he said, *"and if it was possible to move this resolution I should do so: 'That this Standing Joint Committee having received the report of the Sub-Committee, is of the opinion that a more satisfactory conclusion could be arrived at if an independent inquiry was made by the Home Office .....'".*

Radnor was not going to allow this sort of talk! An independent Home Office Inquiry? Who knew what sort of awkward questions they might start to ask? Radnor again shouted George down in mid-sentence:

"I am afraid that I must rule you out of order. You will have to give notice of anything of that kind. I cannot allow it to be read to this meeting."

Reuben George: "*All I can say, my lord, is it is far from a satisfactory conclusion. Had I known when Mr Radcliffe moved his resolution that there was no opportunity of discussing the report clause by clause, I certainly should have spoken at the time. I only thought it would perhaps have been fair to a new member if he had had the opportunity given him of doing so. I have sat on public bodies for many years, and we have always considered a report clause by clause.*"

Radnor: "*I am very sorry, Mr George, as a new member of this Committee feels aggrieved. I think he knew as a member of public bodies I did not feel called upon to warn him of this difficulty in this matter.*"

So Reuben George had been misled by a matter of procedure, which the Earl had conveniently not bothered to alert him to.

Reverend Bardwell now asked if policemen had a right to come before the Standing Joint Committee with grievances.

"*Certainly Not!*" exploded Radnor.

George was beaten, but Bardwell ingenuously continued the line of questioning by stating that he had thought that they had been told at a previous meeting that the right existed, to which Radnor explained that it was a right open to a constable in a borough force to make representation to his Watch Committee, but that no similar right existed in counties. The Earl commented that he had experience of the borough system (as Mayor of Folkestone), and he found it to be irksome.[75]

Everything Wonderful in Wiltshire Constabulary

Llewellyn was now given the opportunity to explain that whenever he carried out an inspection, be gave all his men the opportunity to come before him with grievances, either privately or with their Superintendent. He over-egged the pudding when he told the

---

[75] The reason why borough Police Forces had an appeal system was that many forces were so small that they did not pay the kind of salary which would attract 'gentlemen and born leaders', and it was felt that the decisions of the humbler men who they appointed as Chief Constables should be subject to review by their social superiors. County Chief Constables invariably treated borough Chiefs as socially inferior. Where a borough was policed by the local county force, as at Swindon, the Watch Committee had no right to hear complaints from the county policemen assigned to them.

assembled committee that the force was in such a good state that he had no men with grievances. On this unconvincing note the meeting closed[76].

Two days later a *Salisbury Times* editorial pointed out that the report had effectively upheld the 'one man system' as the opportunity to make recommendations about it had been ignored. In reference to the £52 allowed to Amelia Pike it said, "*On this small grant of a rich authority, the offer of officials of the Police Orphanage to take over the care of two of the children is a rich commentary.*"

Question in the House

On 16th June Mr Thomas Wing, the National Liberal MP for Houghton-le-Spring (Durham) asked in the Commons whether the Home Secretary was aware that the 'One Man System' had resulted in the death of two Wiltshire policemen, by any standards a stunning question. Would the Honourable Gentleman take steps, asked Wing, to remedy what he called "this evil"? The answer given by Sir Ellis Griffiths, Bt. K.C., an under Secretary at the Home Department, was couched in parliamentary language, but amounted to: 'No!'

The shabbiness was not yet quite at an end as the following report from the *Police Review* of 18th July 1913 shows:

---

[76] Mr W. Megaughey of Bournemouth wrote to the author in 2001. He served in Wiltshire police from 1933 to 1958. He says "the only time Llewellyn ever spoke to his men was on passing out parades, and then you could not answer".

> **THE WILTSHIRE TRAGEDY:**
> *We print below a copy of an Appeal that has been circulated throughout the Wiltshire Force:*
>
> *I earnestly appeal to the generosity of the public for subscriptions for the benefit of the widow and children of the late sergeant F. Crouch, who was shot dead on 31st March 1913, while in the execution of his duty.*
>
> *Hoël Llewellyn Chief Constable of Wilts*
>
> Note: This appeal has been delayed in consequence of charges brought against the Chief Constable by the Rev W.W. Keating. The Standing Joint Committee, at the request of the Chief Constable, appointed a special Commission to enquire into the report upon such charges. Their report was presented and adopted by the Standing Joint Committee on 11th June, and states that such charges were entirely without foundation.
>
> *A correspondent writes:* "The one-sidedness of this Appeal is all too apparent. What, indeed has poor Mrs Pike done to be considered outside the pale of Police help? Her husband, we know, on the official report of the S.J.C. Commission, was mad when he committed the crimes for which he has gone to answer to juster Judges than he could get here."

There is no record of any collection for Mrs Pike being authorised within the Wiltshire Force.

Chapter 11

Salt in the Wounds,
October 1913

William Keating's remark a month earlier that the Devizes Inquiry was "the last straw" had been characteristically impetuous, but he cannot be blamed for failing to foresee how readily the S.J.C. would accept the cynically raddled report. Even that was not the final twist, for on 23rd October Captain Llewellyn, who had claimed that his personal honour was under attack from Keating's allegations, was to report to a meeting of the S.J.C. that he had taken legal advice concerning actions for defamation against both Keating and the Editor of the *Wiltshire Gazette*. Both parties, he told the S.J.C. – to Radnor's recorded delight – had agreed to settle out of court by making apologies and paying unspecified costs. Through his remarks to the meeting which be knew would be reported, Llewellyn issued a clear warning that if anything similar happened again he would not be disposed to settle so easily.

The basis of the Chief Constable's complaint against Keating was his 9th April letter to Medlicott, which by Llewellyn's own admission might have been considered to have been covered by qualified privilege had it not been printed in the newspaper. We can see now though that any privilege that Keating might have been able to claim for acting as a priest in the interests of former parishioners would have been undermined by his inclusion of irrelevancies which made him appear vindictive towards Llewellyn. Could it be that the degree of interest shown by the Chief and the Sub-Committee in ensuring that these extraneous allegations were dealt with at length was more than simply a smoke screen, but an aid to Llewellyn should he have launched a libel action?

The poor *Gazette* was badly treated by hearing from Llewellyn's lawyers. Its coverage was referred to as fair and accurate by both sides, and in the immediate aftermath of the deaths they had at first been circumspect about what they chose to print, missing a trick because of it. They only published Keating's letter once his complaints were generally known, and they do seem to have had a fair claim to press privilege which would allow a newspaper to state what a libellous document says, so long as it is within the public domain. Regardless of what they privately thought the truth of the matter to be, both Keating and the newspaper editor would have been wary of receiving a writ from a litigant who had been cleared by an inquiry, and they were probably well advised to apologise and meet small claims for expenses.

Keating's apology, probably penned under legal advice must be seen for what it was, a way of escaping a civil action which he could not hope to successfully oppose. His letter must have been galling for him to write, and equally galling for Ernest Pike's other supporters to read, for it sealed the Chief Constable's victory.

"*TO CAPTAIN HOËL LLEWELLYN, D.S.O.,*

CHIEF CONSTABLE OF WILTS.

Wilsford Vicarage Pewsey,

Wilts   8 October 1913

Sir,

I desire to express my regret that the letter written by me on the 9th April last to Mr Medlicott, as Vice-Chairman of the Standing Joint Committee of the County of Wilts, in reference to the circumstances of the death of P.C. Pike should have appeared on the following morning in the issue of 'Wiltshire Gazette' of the 10th April, and so have given publicity to the allegations affecting yourself before an inquiry into the truth of those allegations had been made. The result of the investigation by the sub-committee appointed by the Wilts Standing Joint Committee into the circumstances has been to entirely exonerate you from the charges which are in such letter against you. I am quite ready to acknowledge that the charges made against you, either expressly or by implication in the letter in question, ought not to have been made, and I ask you to accept my apologies, and to offer as my explanation that my letter was written when under the stress of very strong feeling. You are, of course, at liberty to give such publicity to this letter as you think proper. I am, Sir, Your Obedient Servant."

Earl Radnor expressed his pleasure that the matter had been resolved in so satisfactory a manner to the Chief Constable, and Llewellyn made the necessary arrangements to have the apology widely published.[76]

---

[76] It was at this meeting that the S.J.C. agreed to Llewellyn's request to recompense the cost of dog licences for constables. He waxed lyrical about the abilities of his recommended breeds to sniff out tramps and vagrants, and Reuben George, whilst recognising the value of canine assistance, expressed concern that aggressive dogs should not be set onto poor human creatures.

Chapter 12

Awkward Questions

With the stifling of press comment and of Keating's protests, and the unwillingness of the Home Secretary to become involved, the entire affair was over, and no subsequent criticism has ever been laid at the doors of the Standing Joint Committee or of Hoël Llewellyn until the publication of this book. Local folk memory remembers Ernest Pike as a man who acted as he did because he was thwarted of promotion: a version still advanced in histories supported by the Wiltshire Police. As we have seen, there was far more than that involved.

But the story is not yet quite at an end, for there are still one or two questions to consider.

- Could there have been any basis on which the Chief might have truly thought that there was village gossip about Keating and Amelia Pike? If so, then he could have defended himself against accusations of making scurrilous comment by demonstrating that he was only speaking the truth, but instead he just denied making any comments, and blamed a dead man, Ernest Pike, for dreaming up the story. If the Pike family had been an embarrassment to the village in any way it is very unlikely that the parish council would have eulogised Ernest so generously as they did whilst he was still alive. Nor would they have called for the inquiry if they thought it might reveal a scandal. The Reverend Walter Branfoot could not have been unaware of any shenanigans involving his clerical colleague and personal friend William Keating, especially as his rectory stood very close to Ernest's house on Enford Hill. Keating himself would not have called for an inquiry if he had something to hide.

- Was there any possibility of homosexual attraction between Keating and Pike? Homosexual activity was then a serious crime.

Any suggestion of it could have been investigated by the police. If Ernest had shown even the slightest inclination in this direction he is unlikely to have survived a police career of eighteen years without it becoming known. No police officer had had any qualms about the mens' friendship until Archibald Buchanan arrived in Amesbury, and his reservations about Keating seem to have been based upon resentment about the 1909 Swindon incident. Ernest's remark of 6th March *"They will never separate us,"* and the clergyman's description of their eight year long friendship as '*intimate*' may have connotations to modern ears, but such language would not have been considered unusual in 1913.

Revelations about Keating's behaviour later in life certainly give grounds to be suspicious about his interest in Ernest Pike and other policemen, but there is no reason to suspect that any of them, including Ernest, saw anything more than straightforward friendship in Keating's behaviour.

A Little Firm within a Firm?

The class arrogance of the times honed by the threats to the old order inherent in social changes goes a long way towards explaining why the establishment closed ranks to protect Llewellyn and themselves against proper examination. Perhaps this is enough to fully explain the extraordinarily helpful conduct of the S.J.C. and the coroner towards the Chief Constable. But given that freemasonry has long been suspected of undue influence within certain groups including the police and judiciary, then the masonic credentials of the principal characters involved are a matter of legitimate interest, and failure to consider the subject would undoubtedly generate comment from some of my readers.

In recent years the question of the effect of masonic membership upon policemen and members of the legal profession has been thrown into relief by the investigations of the House of Commons Home Affairs Committee. They have concluded that there is little reason *nowadays* for concern, but they recognise that the culture of secrecy maintained by the Craft contributes to an atmosphere of unease, and have consequently recommended that registers of masonic membership should be compiled.

British freemasonry claims to have taken positive action in the mid-1980s to become much more open, but many modem masonic spokesmen fall into the trap of contrasting a clean image with an earlier, 'murkier' past,[77] and thus tacitly condemn the Brotherhood of their fathers and grandfathers times. Some well-placed non-masonic observers support this view:

"One would sometimes receive instructions regarding one's attitudes to certain people who held prominent positions in public life and had committed infringements of the law. I took this to be a legacy from the old watch committee and standing joint committee days when those governing bodies held the purse strings. It was therefore extremely important for members of the senior police ranks to have close contact, not only in committee, but also socially with such persons who were no doubt closely aligned to the Freemasonry movement."[78]

"In pre-war days it (Freemasonry) was a power to be reckoned with in the Police Force....."[79]

For an even earlier comment, contemporaneous with the events in this book, there is this, from the *Police Review* in 1913:

"SECRET SOCIETIES"

"A correspondent who takes a deep practical interest in the Police, and indeed in all efforts for the uplifting of his fellow men, and who would be the last

---

[77] See House of Commons Home Affairs committee report into Freemasonry in Judiciary and Police (HMSO 1997). Police federation evidence stated that *'the force of today is far more open and accountable than 20 or 30 years ago, when a number of police scandals (some allegedly involving the masons) took place'*.
Sir Ian Percival QC for the Law Society, and himself a mason, stressed that Freemasonry has *'recently at least* worked hard to assure that those who abused the organisation were disciplined' (Author's italics).

[78] Article by Sgt Peter Wellings, Nottinghamshire Constabulary, *'Police Review'* May 1972. Wellings is not a freemason.

[79] From article by Brian Clark, sometime Editor *'Police Review'*.

man to induce the Police or any other class to join any society for promoting or sanctioning wrong doing, complains that the Police Instruction Book of his County contains an order prohibiting a constable from belonging to any political society or to any secret society except that of the Freemasons. Our friend takes no exception to Freemasonry, but wonders why that society is singled out. The rule seems absurd on the face of it, and breathes a spirit of suspicion and domination that cannot conduce to good feeling."[80]

In the nineteenth and early twentieth centuries upper and middle class men found the idea of freemasonry, with its royal connections, an attractive proposition, and aspired to initiation. Many, whilst maintaining the secrets of the Craft, were quite open about the fact of their membership, but even so, establishing the identity of pre-First World War Wiltshire freemasons has not been particularly easy. Nevertheless, I have been able to satisfy myself that the Wiltshire magistracy of 1913 was thoroughly riddled with masons.

My research has revealed very few police members though, and in particular, I can find no positive connection for Hoël Llewellyn; someone named Llewellyn joined a Wiltshire Lodge in the year that Hoël arrived in the county, but this may be a coincidence.

Inquiries at the United Grand Lodge of England, and the Grand Lodges of Scotland and Ireland have also drawn blanks. This should not be considered conclusive though, as the misleading performance of the Grand Scribe of U.G.L.E. before a parliamentary committee demonstrated as recently as 1997. His claim that no, present-day Chief Constables belonged to the Craft was revealed as inaccurate when contradictory – and correct – information was provided by the Association of Chief Police Officers.[81]

Of those in particular positions to assist Llewellyn, Lord Radnor was a senior mason, as were his predecessors as chairman of the S.J.C. Sir

---
[80] In fairness, it should be pointed out that freemasons object to the use of any terminology suggesting that theirs is a 'secret' society.
[81] 'On The Square' or not though, Llewellyn certainly received considerable assistance from men who were masons, and not only in connection with the Coombe affair. His application to join the army at the outbreak of war in 1914, an honourable thing to do, was helped enormously and specifically by intervention by two very senior freemasons.

John Goldney a member of the Inquiry Commission, belonged to what must have been the most prominent masonic family in Wiltshire, and Coroner Sylvester had been initiated into the Trowbridge Lodge of Concord (No. 632) in 1901. The Wiltshire M.P.s, all Conservative, who left the responsibility of raising a parliamentary question to a Durham Liberal, were all county J.P.s and Freemasons.

Well, well, well . . . .

In March 1912 a husband and wife named Seddon were tried at the Old Bailey for the murder of their wealthy lodger, Eliza Barrow. The case is well known, and features in the *Notable British Trials* series. Attorney General Sir Rufus Issacs prosecuted, and Edward Marshall Hall, arguably the most flamboyant barrister that the English Bar has produced, defended. Mrs Seddon was found not guilty, but her husband was condemned by strong circumstantial evidence, not helped by his arrogance in court. The insurance manager had slowly poisoned the spinster with an arsenic solution dissolved from fly papers, leaving her to suffer alone in the most filthy and squalid fashion. Once the verdict was in, there was only one course open to the judge, and he began customarily:

"*Frederick Henry Seddon, have you anything to say why sentence of death should not be passed upon you?*"

"*I have, my lord,*" said the doomed man, drawing his hand across his brow in a masonic sign of distress, and staring the judge fixedly in the eye:

" ..... *I declare by the Great Architect of the Universe that I am not guilty.*"[82]

The effect upon his Honour was electric, for he too was a freemason, being the Provincial Grand Master for Surrey. Despite his distress, obvious to all in court, the solemn preparations for pronouncements of the only possible penalty went ahead; the black cap was placed on his wig, and the court doors locked.

---

[82] The Times, 15th March 1912.

AWKWARD QUESTIONS

Silence was called for by the Court Usher, but the judge then sat for a full, agonising speechless minute before he could bring himself to utter the dread sentence on a fellow mason.

He had sent many men to the drop before, but when he did manage to begin his short address to the loathsome Seddon he was visibly in the grip of the most intense emotion, and his voice was at times inaudible. Shaking with tears, and with painfully long silences in his delivery, he acknowledged that they both belonged to the Brotherhood, but he reminded Seddon that the Craft required obedience to the state's law.

There was little hope of appeal or reprieve for the man in the dock, for the evidence was strong, poisoners received scant sympathy and the judge advised the Home Secretary that he thought the result of the trial was correct. Hangman John Ellis duly obliged society and the pungent shade of Eliza Barrow by sending Seddon to make his own explanations to the Great Architect via the gallows trap at HM Prison Pentonville at 9.00 a.m. on 18th April 1912.

It's a well-known story, but what place has it here? Firstly, it shows that despite declarations of altruistic aims, men who are prepared to try and use the Craft for their own ends find it all too easy to join. But there are many such instances — why relate this one?

Well, Seddon's weeping judge was none other than Sir Thomas Townsend Bucknill, who, helped by the strangely submissive pliability of barrister Mr Clavell Salter, had gone to such lengths to stop the trial of Ernest Pike at Salisbury Assizes in April 1902.[83]

---

[83] One of the best descriptions of Bucknill's behaviour at the Seddon trial may be found in the biography of a junior member of the prosecution team. See *The Life and Cases of Mr Justice Humphreys*' by Stanley Jackson (Odhams Press, ND, pp 92-105).

Chapter 13

Aftermath
1913-2013

Why did the concern and the outrage subside so quickly? Of all the people who had expressed concern – Keating, Kempster, George, Hanks, Morse, the Enford Parish Council – was there not one who persisted? The answer was no, and there would seem to be a number of reasons:

- After the matter had been inquired into, no matter how prejudiced the proceedings, the complainants would have despaired of achieving any success.

- Llewellyn's readiness to sue was obvious. He had silenced Keating and the press by the threat of litigation, and issued a warning that he would come down harder if any party repeated the allegations against him. Kempster realised that the battle had been lost, for in the *Police Review* of 7th November 1913 he had this to say:

    "This sad incident embracing the murder of one constable by another, and the suicide of his murderer, has recently been followed locally by some steps to establish the complete immunity of the Chief Constable from any blame. The Rev W.W. Keating who published certain complaints of P.C. Pike against the Chief Constable has, we believe, conveyed to that gentleman an expression of his full acquiescence in his entire exoneration by the Standing Joint Committee. Mr Keating's charges as published after the double fatality must have caused great pain to the Chief Constable as to any right minded man under such painful circumstances. It would seem almost inevitable that every incident contributory to so tragic an event must gain publicity through the press, but as the newspaper press in reporting a coroner's inquest and otherwise is the indispensable instrument of such publicity so should it also emphasise, if possible, those findings which tend to remove any unjust reflection it may have assisted to make known.

> *For ourselves we have no hesitation in expressing deep regret that the Chief Constable should have been caused any suffering by the publication of charges made by a deceased constable whose mind was deranged, which charges have been proved to be absolutely untrue. We are glad to believe Mr. Keating also has acquiesced in entirely absolving the Chief Constable from any possible blame or discredit: and we would enjoin upon our readers whose sympathies, like our own, may very easily carry toward what for the moment may appear the weaker side, to dismiss from their minds any suspicion that the Chief Constable acted towards Pike otherwise than with the utmost consideration of his case. Whilst we are usually occupied in the defence of the subordinate, it is no less our duty to maintain respect for the highest in authority, and in this case that respect and sympathy are eminently due to the Chief Constable of Wiltshire."*

A very elegantly written apology, for sure, but what had happened to bring such a change of heart about? Surely the findings of the Devizes Inquiry were not so convincing, for the *Police Review* had criticised its partial constitution even before it reported its findings. No magazine proprietor would want to back down in such a public way, and given that there had been no new revelations to account for the magazine's *volte face*, the apology is too obsequious to be accepted at face value. The suspicion must surely be that it had been written under pressure of legal advice. Expediency rather than sincerity must be the motive underlying this apology.

- Developments in the Pike family were another factor that would tend to dampen any further protest. Ernest's elderly parents, Oliver and Susannah, had had a distressing time even before the killings at Coombe, with two of the elder sons emigrating, so the very siblings who might have been expected to take the leading part in representing the family's interests were far across the seas. The circumstances of Ernest's death were the last straw for the old man, and he died suddenly a month after the Report's publication.[84] Amelia Pike did not want the matter to be kept in the public eye.

---

[84] Obit. Wiltshire and Gloucester Standard 26th July 1913.

- Within months, the Great War had started, and the dreadful harvest of death made individual mortality pale into insignificance. In the face of such large scale suffering so nobly endured, it would have been worse than indelicate for anybody to have tried to focus attention on the squalid deaths of Frank Crouch and Ernest Pike.

- As the war finished, massive loss of life continued with the global influenza pandemic. When this passed there was an overwhelming sense that the world had changed irreversibly, and the old pre-war days seemed to belong to a distant, different past. Gradually the facts of the Coombe killings began to be forgotten.

- As the focal point of remonstration in 1913, William Keating needed personal credibility if he was going to achieve any success. He bodged the job almost from the start, and his subsequent climb down was very damaging. But if he, or anybody else, kept any faint hope of reawakening his protests once the war was over, they were dealt a crushing blow when the old vicar's reputation was finally completely ruined in early 1920.

As the war approached its end things finally started to change within the police. At an S.J.C. meeting on 17th October 1918 Mr C. Hill, a County Councillor on the committee, moved a proposition that a right of appeal to the S.J.C. should be given to constables, and that they should be permitted to be accompanied by an officer of their choice at any hearing. He was seconded by – who else? – Reuben George, but the motion was withdrawn after it had been agreed that a sub-committee should look into the matter. Hill's proposition was not an independent initiative, but had been prompted by a Home Office letter of 18th September which requested police authorities to consider such measures in the aftermath of a strike in the Metropolitan Police. The sub-committee met on 10th January 1919, and reported on the 23rd following when it was decided to set up a 'Wiltshire Police Representative Board' which could make representations to the Chief

AFTERMATH

Constable on all matters of welfare and conditions of service *other than discipline*.

Intriguingly this all coincided with Llewellyn's return from War Service on 19th January, and after a meeting at Trowbridge on 10th March 1919 the first delegation approached the Chief Constable on 27th March to ask that sergeants and constables should live rent free.

The Government had been forced to consider the state of morale within the police, for the prospect of large scale civil disorder was a very real one. Great swathes of the population were no longer prepared to accept the old pre-war order, and the Bolshevik Revolution in Russia provided a chilling model for how they might change things. Troops were unsettled, and leave men sometimes had to be forced to rejoin their units in France at gunpoint. Canadian soldiers waiting for ships home rioted at Kimnel Park Camp near Rhyl and killed a military policeman, and others killed a sergeant of the Surrey Constabulary on Derby Day 17th June 1919.[85] The police union that had been in uneasy, clandestine existence for some years organised a short strike of the Metropolitan Force in 1918 and called for action by other forces. When the Liverpool Force came out on 1st August 1919 warships were sent to the Mersey. Thousands of policemen were sacked, and Llewellyn warned his own men that he would act similarly, and would not permit any dismissed constable to rejoin the force, no matter what the outcome of any negotiations might be. He would see to it that they would lose their pension rights too, and he was believed.

In view of the spectre of large scale refusals by the police to keep the peace, a committee under Lord Desborough was formed which recommended the rapid enactment of sweeping changes, many of which had been proposed in the abortive 1913 Bill. In May 1919 Home Secretary Edward Shortt sought leave to introduce a Police Bill, and on 8th July the 1919 Police Act was passed into law.

---

[85] The circumstances of this killing were suppressed for political reasons. A full account may be found in 'The Murder of Sergeant Thomas Green at Epsom Police Station' by Edward Shortland (privately published, Chessington, 1996).

The Police Federation was formed, drawing the teeth from the unions, and amongst welcome provisions of the Act, a uniform disciplinary code and rights of appeal in all forces were finally introduced. But the reactionaries in Wiltshire were not going to give up their old ways easily. In January 1920 Llewellyn reported to the S.J.C. that his force was undermanned. When it was pointed out that dismissals were a significant contributory factor to the shortage, Reuben George said that the committee should be made aware of the reasons policemen were being sacked. Lord Radnor was not going to allow this sort of thing though, and ruled that discretion in matters of dismissals must remain entirely in the hands of the Chief Constable.[86]

PEOPLE AND PLACES

The People

The Widows and Children. Both widows struggled to bring up their children as best they could, and neither ever remarried. Alice (Kate) Crouch was strict with her two fatherless boys, Wilfred and Leslie, and in photographs they were always immaculately and identically dressed. Neither ever married. Alice died in Trowbridge on 28th May 1956 at the age of 80, and was interred in her husband's grave. Leslie died in May 1985, and Wilfred passed away in November 1992 at the age of 88. Both sons are buried close to their parent's grave. Wilfred's will caused a local sensation, for he left £180,000 to the church where his parents lie buried.

Amelia Pike returned to live in Malmesbury. Walter Branfoot, the Enford vicar helped her to find work as a teacher, and with assistance from her family she managed to get by. In due course, she received some property, two houses, as a legacy. Daughters Dorothy and Gladys, aged eleven and ten were sent to the Police Orphanage at Reigate, an experience which they bitterly remembered throughout their lives (Dorothy died in 1962, Gladys in 1990).

---

[86] S.J.C. Minutes, 22nd January 1920.

Enford folk showed true compassion to the shattered family though, and Dorothy returned there to marry a villager in 1925, and years later her children found wartime refuge there from the bombing of Southampton where they had settled. No mention of their grandfather's tragedy was ever made to them and it was only on the night of Dorothy's death in 1962 that her children were finally told the truth.

The six Pike children would eventually produce sixteen grandchildren, all of whom were shielded to some extent from the facts, at least until they reached maturity. Even when the truth was revealed to them it was confined to the basic facts, and those whom I tracked down and contacted during my research were unaware of the despicable way in which their grandparents had been treated by the county police authorities. Amelia died in 1959 aged eighty five and is buried in Malmesbury.

Thomas Morse, Amelia's brother in law who had tried so hard to help her, became mayor of Malmesbury in 1936.

Reverend William Wrixon Keating divested himself of responsibility for the parish of Manningford Bohune in mid-1913, but stayed as Vicar of Wilsford. By 1920 he was suffering from arteriolsclerosis and displaying signs of senility. Unfortunately he had become a figure of ridicule to some of the more unpleasant young residents of his parish, a state of affairs to which he contributed in some ways, not least by his vanity of dying his beard.

In September 1919 he discussed retirement with the Bishop of Salisbury, and in light of subsequent events it is sad that he did not act immediately, for in early February 1920 he was arrested on six charges of indecency involving youths, and was remanded briefly in custody. When he was brought before a special session of Pewsey magistrates on 11th February, solicitors on both sides requested proceedings to be held *in camera*. It was within the powers of magistrates conducting committal proceedings to allow this, but the application was refused by the Bench. Keating's public humiliation was given a turn of the screw when his old antagonist Superintendent Archibald Buchanan gave evidence. The Bench committed the old vicar for trial at Assize, and released him on bail.

On 30th May 1920 William Keating took his trial before Mr Justice Bray at Salisbury. Thomas Henning Parr prosecuted; we last came across him representing Llewellyn at Devizes, but now he was Recorder of Salisbury, and would go on to take silk in 1922. The defence team were particularly talented, being led by Holman Gregory, who had been Clavell Salter's junior at Pike's perjury trial. By now Gregory was a Member of Parliament, and he would go on to become Common Serjeant and Recorder of London. The other barrister for Keating was the Recorder of Poole, Rayner Goddard, who would one day become Lord Chief Justice of England.

The case was a sordid one. Although Keating pleaded not guilty, there was no denying that a disgusting incident had occurred in the drive of the Wilsford Vicarage after evening service at St Nicholas's on Sunday 25th January 1920, but the evidence conflicted over the matter of who initiated it, and whether it had been welcomed.

Goddard presented his client as a frail old man in the throes of a second childhood, a sympathetic image which he created so successfully that the judge went some way to counter it in his summing up. A verdict of 'Not Guilty' was returned and William Keating went free, though it was now beyond question that his days as a serving clergyman were at an end. His parishioners had already shown what they thought by staying away from his services, and Walter Branfoot had stepped in *pro temps*.

Soon afterwards the Reverend Charles Hewitt was appointed to the parish, and Keating, abandoned by most of the friends he had made in his forty years in Wiltshire went into retirement in Bournemouth, living firstly in a hotel at 4 Grove Road. His request to relinquish his living, held by Wiltshire County Archives, is unusually completed in red ink by the Diocesan Solicitor, an indication of the unusual circumstances of his departure. He died at 3 North Lodge Road,

Branksome near Poole on Sunday 10th December 1922 at the age of 76 and was buried in Wilsford on Friday 15th December 1922 at 2.30 p.m. The principal officiating chaplain was his old friend Walter Branfoot, still vicar of Enford, and now also Rural Dean, assisted by the Reverends Sutton of nearby North Newnton, and Hewitt, Keating's successor at Wilsford.

There is little trace today of the striking Irishman who served the little Wiltshire parish for 40 years; there is no recollection of him in the village, nor any sort of memorial in the church. The stained glass memorial to his mother, who died in 1895, has little meaning to today's congregations, and the two graves are not marked.[87] Unusually, the Salisbury Diocesan Almanack and Gazette, which published obituaries until the mid-1930s, did not commemorate this priest who had served the See of Salisbury for so long. (In contrast, Branfoot, who died a little over three years later on 10th February 1926, received a generous tribute despite having served the diocese for only fifteen years).[88] By accident or design the memory of this odd, turbulent, Irish priest has now been all but obliterated.

Hoël Llewellyn applied to join the Army on the outbreak of war in 1914, despite being of an age when he might honourably have stayed in Wiltshire. He specifically asked to join the 3rd County of London Yeomanry, and to support his application his stunning testimonials were again wheeled out – he had gone to the trouble of having them printed.

This time he was also personally recommended by Field Marshal Lord Methuen, now Chairman of the Territorial Association. The two men met at the Corn Exchange in Devizes on the evening of 29th August 1914, and Llewellyn followed up with a letter to the Field Marshal the following morning. Methuen had openly declared that he would not use his influence to advance the applications of individuals, but

---

[87] There is no churchyard plan for Wilsford, but the author believes that he has identified the site of Keating's grave.
[88] Obit. Branfoot, Salisbury Diocesan Gazette, March 1926.

pointedly made an exception in Llewellyn's case, writing directly to the Military Secretary.[89] (Methuen was a very prominent Freemason). Less than a week later, as the first indications of heavy casualties from the Battle of Mons were being received in England, it was reported that the Chief Constable was to join the Colours and by 19th September he was back in khaki with the temporary rank of Major.[90] At a secret meeting of the S.J.C. on 11th December 1914 it was agreed that the Chief Constable's army salary (£274 p.a.) should be topped up from county funds to the amount of his Chief Constable's earnings which totalled £771.

By August 1915 Llewellyn's regiment was based at Moascar near Ismailia on the Suez Canal. Desperate calls for reinforcements for Gallipoli on the 14th resulted in them being rapidly reorganised as infantry, and they were transported via Alexandria and Mudros to the fiasco at Suvla Bay, landing from H.M.S. *'Doris'* at 5.30 on the morning of 18th August. Two days later they were deployed for a general assault, and at 3.30 on the afternoon of 21st August they went into action. Immediately upon leaving their positions they were caught by intense artillery fire as the entire 2nd Mounted (Yeomanry) Division made a gallant advance across the smooth white surface of a dried up salt lake, and Llewellyn, together with 40 of his men, was very quickly hit.

He was luckier than many. He lived, and his wound, a longitudinal piercing of the left foot by shrapnel was officially classified as 'severe but not permanent'. Furthermore, he was to be spared the ordeal of admission into one of the military hospitals in Egypt or Malta where death rates from secondary infection were extraordinarily high, for on 13th August they had all been reported full, and so he was invalided directly home on H.M. Hospital Ship *'Soudan'*, disembarking at Plymouth on 3rd September 1915. After a few days in St Thomas's

---

[89] Letters in Llewellyn's War Office file, Public Record Office WO 374/42480.
[90] A number of county Chief Constables rejoined the army in 1914, leading the *Police Review* to ask in 1918 whether they were really necessary, as their forces had all run perfectly well without them (see P.R. 1918 p 229).

Hospital in London he was sent on sick leave to recover, and by November he was passed as fit to return to service despite a metal splash on his scaphoid bone and some residual tenderness when walking over uneven ground.

In January 1916 he embarked from Devonport and shortly afterwards took up the appointment of Provost Marshal (the senior Military Policeman) of the Egyptian Expeditionary Force in the rank of Lieutenant Colonel. He spent much of the next two years on the move around the garrison areas of Cairo, Ismailia and Alexandria.[91] With the collapse of Turkish resistance in the Middle East, he contrived to transfer to the newly established Tank Corps on the Western Front. He left Egypt on 11th August 1918 aboard H.M.T. Indurra and after a course at Bovington, Dorset, he crossed to France on 16th October arriving at Bermicourt the following day, where he was destined for command of the 9th Tank Battalion, a Heavy unit equipped with the latest Mark V crawlers. The previous C.O., Lt.Col M.K.K. Woods had left to command 2nd Tank Brigade. On the very day of Llewellyn's arrival, 9th Battalion was ordered into its last battle of the war, Fôret de Mormal. The Second in Command, Major Butler, was appointed to command instead of the inexperienced Llewellyn. The Armistice came, and he was ordered home and demobilised remarkably quickly, leaving France on 27th November, and resuming active command of the Wiltshire Police from Robert Buchanan on 19th January 1919.[92]

In December, during the post war distribution of honours amongst the victorious nations, he collected the green and white insignia of the Italian Order of St. Maurice and St. Lazarus.[93] Llewellyn's birthplace, Langford Court which had been let since the death of his mother in 1906 had eventually been sold out of the family shortly after the death of his father in 1914.[94]

---

[91] Llewellyn earned a Mention in Field Marshal Allenby's despatches on 16th January 1918.
[92] Force General Order. 188, 23rd January 1919.
[93] Force General Order. 186, 16th December 1918.
[94] The house and estate had thus been in possession of the Llewellyn family for only one generation. It was sold to Sir George Wills of the tobacco dynasty.

Winifred Llewellyn died in 1931, and at about this time Hoël was appointed as Deputy Lieutenant for the county of Wiltshire. In 1933 he married Constance Mary Morley at a ceremony in Chelsea, a daughter of the Sandeman port vintner's family, who like Winifred was a divorcée. There were no offspring of either of his marriages, but Constance Morley brought him a family of step children.

During the course of Hitler's War the Salisbury City Police amalgamated with the County Constabulary, and against Llewellyn's wishes policewomen were recruited into the force. He was County Civil Defence Controller from the early days of the war, and although the county was not in the front line of the Blitz it was crammed with British and American troops, and German prisoners, all of whom caused difficulties for the police. His position as England's senior Chief Constable, and his wartime efforts (it is said that he never took a day off during the war) were rewarded by a knighthood in 1943, but on 20th March 1945 the 73 year old warrior finally gave notice that due to his state of health he would retire on the 24th June. Before he could do so, he died in harness on the 2nd April, one week short of having completed 37 years' service as Chief Constable.

Hoël Llewellyn's remains were cremated in Bristol on 5th April and his ashes returned to the church near his birthplace in Burrington, Somerset, where a number of his relatives, including his first wife Winifred, lie buried. His memory was commemorated next day at a service held in St. Johns Church, Devizes which was attended by eight Chief Constables, and later by a brass plaque which was placed under the Second World War Roll of Honour at the old Police H.Q. in Bath Road Devizes.

The plaque, in the form of the Llewellyn family crest a Paschal Lamb bearing the motto 'Ym Gwlad' (For My Country), was subsequently located in the entrance of Llewellyn House, an accommodation block at the present County Police Headquarters until the demolition of the building. Memorials to Sir Hoël, both of his wives and other family members may also be found in Holy Trinity Church at Burrington.

AFTERMATH

Some artefacts of Llewellyn's military service have survived in unlikely places; an unusual long barrelled pattern Mk V Webley revolver, purchased from the Army and Navy store in London by men of the Constabulary, inscribed appropriately and presented to him when he left for war service, is still lodged in the Wiltshire Police armoury.

In 1963 a Royal Army Ordnance Corps captain contacted the Metropolitan Police to seek assistance in disposing of a ceremonial sword of colonial police pattern which had been found abandoned in an old office at the Ministry of Defence.

For the next quarter of a century the sword remained with the police officer to whom it had been passed. After his retirement, and during a visit to the Metropolitan Police Mounted Branch Museum, it was mentioned that the then Commissioner, the late Sir Kenneth Newman, had no ceremonial sword to wear, and so it was passed to the Commissioner's Groom. This gentleman (a police constable) made enquiries which revealed that the sword had originally been made for Hoël Llewellyn when he was a District Commandant in the South African Constabulary.

Llewellyn's stepson from his marriage to Constance Morley gave permission for the sword to be retained by the police. It was refurbished by the original makers, Metropolitan Police motifs replacing those of the SAC, and has since 1988 been used by the Commissioners of the Metropolitan Police whenever grand ceremonial duties have required it.

Llewellyn's medals came up for sale in the 1980s and were purchased in good faith by a retired member of the British South Africa Police resident in Rhodesia / Zimbabwe. His enquiries led him in due course to the same generous stepson who had agreed to give the sword to the Metropolitan Police, and it transpired that the medals had, in fact, been stolen some time earlier. In an act of gentlemanly generosity, and seeing that the medals could not be in more appropriate hands, the stepson gave up any claim to ownership and agreed that undisputed ownership should rest with the Rhodesian possessor.

Some other policemen. Frank Crouch was replaced as station sergeant at Netheravon by Sgt. James Jones on 19th April 1913. Five days later P.C. William Slade, the first policeman on the scene of Crouch's killing was promoted sergeant and replaced at Upavon by P.C. Albert Symonds. Not until 27th May though did Irishman Danny McGrath move from Swindon's Telford Road Station to become Ernest Pike's successor as the Enford bobby.

Thomas Robinson retired at the age of 57 at the end of April 1914, and Robert Buchanan replaced him as Deputy Chief Constable, an appointment that brought him considerable responsibility during the Great War. He retired in 1923 being replaced as DCC by Superintendent Brooks who had been another one of those present at the incident with the whisky at the Swindon police cricket club in February 1909. Robert Buchanan junior, the constable who worked alongside his father at the Devizes Police H.Q. was one of those who left to join the army on the outbreak of the Great War and did not return to the force.

Archibald Buchanan earned two commendations during the Great War, one directly from the Home Secretary. Like his older brother he also retired in 1923 and bought a bungalow in Edwards Road Amesbury, within a stone's throw of the Police Station. He died in Oswestry, Shropshire, in 1943 aged 70.

Inspector Mark Elkins of Ludgershall who attended the scene of the deaths and the inquest, and who was almost certainly the officer who called Amelia to the inquest, retired in April 1915 with a pension of just under £75 per annum. He then ran a garage business in Ludgershall. As a man who had himself fallen foul of the 'one-man system', he was given a generous testimonial in the pages of the *Police Review*.

P.C. Wilson, the first policeman to see Ernest's body has not had the national recognition he deserves for his part in the introduction of dogs into police service. He owned Shadower, the sire of Moonlight and Flair, whilst stationed at Ogbourne St. George near Marlborough.

Wilson resigned from the Wiltshire Constabulary in May 1914 and went to Scotland as a trainer of sporting dogs.

Captain Robert Sterne R.N. who was Chief Constable at the time of the Race Plain affair died in 1926 and is buried at Potterne near Devizes.

Jacob Pleydell-Bouverie, 6th Earl of Radnor, of Longford Castle, Salisbury, family motto 'Patria Cara Carior Liberta' (My Country is Dear: Liberty is Dearer) was Commanding Officer of the 4th (Territorial) Battalion) of the Wiltshire Regiment, and went with them to India in the Great War, Medlicott deputising once more as chairman of the S.J.C. Radnor was promoted to Brigadier and assumed an appointment on the staff of the Dehra Dun brigade of the Indian army. He became Lord Lieutenant of Wiltshire in 1925, a post he held until his death at the age of 61 on 25th June 1930.

Eustace Green, the butcher beaten at the Salisbury races died in his home village of Sutton Mandeville in January 1934, aged 59.

The Inquiry Commissioners

Mr Francis Reynolds Yonge Radcliffe K. C., chairman of the Devizes inquiry and principal author of the report, left Wiltshire in 1914 to become a judge on the Oxfordshire and Northamptonshire circuit. He died in 1924.

Henry Edmonstone Medlicott, of Potterne died at the age of 76 on 6th September 1916 after experiencing the loss on active service of his youngest son, a Royal Naval Air Service officer. The Marquis of Bath then took over the chair of the S.J.C. until Radnor's return from active service.

Sir John Tankerville Goldney died at his home in Wiltshire on 11th April 1920.

Reuben George died on 4th June 1936, three months before his 72nd birthday and was buried at Radnor Street Cemetery, Swindon. A much loved resident of the town he was the subject of a commemorative booklet published by the Swindon Evening Advertiser:

*"We do not think that Reuben George had a single enemy, though many times he differed profoundly from most of his County Council and Swindon Town Council colleagues. There was not an atom of malice in the man. All men were his brothers. He was a champion of minorities."*95

Who could wish for a better epitaph than that?

Frederick Arthur Percy Sylvester retired as HM Coroner about 1920 and went to live in Frome Road, Bradford on Avon, then later in Victoria Road Trowbridge. His family practise is still one of the principal legal firms in the town.

Harry Harding. Life returned to normal for only a short time for the groom who gave evidence to the inquiry about recovering Ernest Pike's body. His brothers, both regulars in the 1st Battalion of the Wiltshire Regiment were dead within two months of the outbreak of war, falling together near Neuve Chapelle in October 1914. Harry joined up at Bulford Camp, but it was not long before Last Post rang out over his grave too.96

Harry had served as a Driver in the Royal Field Artillery in the Boer War, being present at a famous action at Colenso when several Victoria Crosses were won for attempts to save some abandoned guns. He won the Distinguished Conduct Medal at Kimberley in February 1900 for bringing his gun into action single handedly, driving only the two wheeler gun horses after the rest of the six horse team had been killed by Boer fire. It seems that he did not mention this gallant conduct when he re-enlisted in 1914, for neither his service records nor his war grave record the fact that he held the DCM, though it is mentioned on a family memorial in Netheravon churchyard. After losing all three sons in the war, his broken hearted father died in 1917, and a sister, Charity, died in February 1919, probably of influenza. Unbelievable as it may seem, some other valley families were hit even harder by the War and its aftermath. Little

---

95 Swindon Evening Advertiser, 5th June 1936.
96 Lance Corporal Harry Harding, died 20th August 1915, is interred at Chatby Military Cemetery, Alexandria.

wonder then, that any idea of reopening the matter of the Coombe deaths had little appeal.

Mrs Ivy Punter who recalled being told that "*Wilfred would not be at school today*", became the Netheravon schoolmistress for over 50 years, and was the last local person who had any personal recollection, be it ever so slight, of the events of the night of 31st March 1913. She died aged 97 in April 1999.

The Places, the Sites Today

The locations of the incidents have altered little, thanks to the military ownership of most of the land, though some 1913 sight lines are now different due to vegetation growth or felling.

The Murder Site. Coombe cross roads, roughly aligned with the cardinal points of the compass would still be recognised by Crouch and Pike. The farm buildings on the north eastern quarter of the junction where Frank Crouch's body was laid out were demolished in the early 1990s and replaced by houses, though the Victorian post box in which Ernest Pike may have posted his last letters is still in place being built into a new stone wall. Shortly after the Second World War a concrete tank track was laid which covered part of the old footpath by which Sgt Crouch approached the scene of his death. The narrow sunken lane from Fittleton still descends Bamber Hill between the high earth banks that provided Ernest Pike's probable hiding place. The elms near the murder site are gone: several fell in a storm in 1928, the remainder succumbing to disease in the 1980s. In July 2000 the author erected a small brass memorial to both men on the southern garden wall of Coombe Farmhouse, by kind permission of the present owners. It is within a few yards of the spot where Frank Crouch died.

The Suicide Site is almost identical to how it was in 1913, although the footbridge was replaced by a new one in 2010.

The Inquest Courtroom is now a drawing room in the farm house, which is externally unchanged.

The Three Horse Shoes was owned by Hussey's Netheravon Brewery at the time of the affair, but in June 1913 it was one of 23 premises which the local firm sold off and Ushers Brewery acquired it. Walter Phillimore kept the pub until the late 1920s. It has been a private house for many years and is now called 'Three Horse Shoes Cottage'.

The Red Lion, Chisenbury is externally little changed. Little Arch, where Ernest Pike may have exchanged greetings with Walter Phillimore is about 50 yards from the pub in the direction of Enford.

Littlecott House, which Ernest claimed to have checked on his way back from Chisenbury, was in process of sale to the Army in 1913. It was used as a residence by senior officers of all three services for many years.

The Policemen's houses. Ernest Pike's cottage still stands, now named 'Peelers Cottage'. Frank Crouch's brick and flint house is recognisable at the southern end of Netheravon High Street. A permanent police presence was withdrawn from Enford before the Second World War, and two bobbies were then stationed at Netheravon in new accommodation and so both houses reverted to their landlords.

The Amesbury Police Station. The Amesbury Police Division ceased to exist in 1943 when it became a part of the Salisbury Division as a consequence of the amalgamation of the City and County forces. The impressive building in School Lane was occupied by the Police until 1961, and is now private residences.

The Graves. The remains of William Frank Crouch and his widow lie in Rowde churchyard near Devizes. His impressive headstone informs all who may read it that he was killed on duty.

Ernest Pike's resting place is in the churchyard at Enford. The four wheeled bier which carried his coffin can still be seen inside the church. One of the coffin bearers was a local man named Jos. Carter who provided many services to the church. Twelve years later his son married Dorothy Pike, one of Earnest's daughters who had been sent to the Reigate Police Orphanage. Her children therefore had a paternal grandfather who carried their maternal grandfather to the grave. Ernest's headstone bears no inscription other than his name and date of death. If he needs an epitaph then perhaps it might be these words from the final passage from the Litany spoken at his funeral:

From our enemies defend us O Christ,
Graciously look upon our afflictions

ACKNOWLEDGEMENTS AND SOURCES

Sources already mentioned in text footnotes may not be repeated below. Not all acknowledged contributors will agree with or approve of my conclusions. Some helped; others did no more than acknowledge receipt of a letter.

Nevertheless, I am grateful to them all.

Books:

The Netheravon Police Murder is briefly mentioned in the following books:

Oldest and Best by Paul Sample, No Limmits Public Relations 1989.
Blue Murder, Policemen under Suspicion by Joan Lock, Hale 1986.

Over the years I have been fascinated by this case, I have consulted a vast number of books, amongst which were the following:

Coronership by G Thurston, Barry Rose, London 1980
Jervis on the Office and Duties of Coroners, Sweet and Maxwell, various editions.
Open Verdict by E A Williams MBE, Oyez Publications 1967
The British Police. Police Forces and Chief Officers 1829 - 2000 by Stallion and Wall. Police History Society 1999.
The Official Encyclopaedia of Scotland Yard, Fido and Skinner, Virgin Books 1999.
History of the Police in England and Wales, T A Critchley, Constable 1967.
The English Police. Political and Social History by C Emsley St Martin's Press 1991.
The Freemason's Pocket Reference Book by F L Pick and Norman Wright, Fred Muller London 1955.
The Royal Masonic Cyclopaedia, Kenneth Mackenzie, London 1887
History of Freemasonry in Wiltshire by Francis Hastings Goldney, private, 1880.
The British Society 1914-45 by John Stevenson, Penguin Books 1984.

ACKNOWLEDGEMENTS AND SOURCES

The Harmsworth Encyclopaedia, 1906
Police Law by CCH Moriarty, Butterworth and Co 1929.
Jowitts Dictionary of Law, Sweet and Maxwell, London 1926.
The Matabele Campaign 1896 by RSS Baden-Powell, Methuen 1897.
Die Beleg van Mafeking, reproduced in translation in *Rhodesia Served the Queen* by Col AS Hickman, Government Printer, Salisbury Rhodesia 1970.
The Jameson Raid by J van der Poel, Oxford University Press 1951.
With Plumer in Matabeleland, by P W Sykes, Constable 1897.
Hansard, June 1913.
Somerset Leaders by Ernest Gaskell, privately published no date, circa 1906.
The History of the Royal Navy (Vol 7) by Sir William Laird Clowes, Sampson Low Marston 1903.
Directories: *Burke ('Landed Gentry', 'Peerage') Kelly's* (Regional and 'Official and Titled Classes'). *Gillimans Public Registers, Crockfords Clerical Registers. Who Was Who*.

Although published too late to be useful in my research, '*Chief Constables of England and Wales: A Socio-Legal History of Criminal Justice Elite*' by David S Wall, (Ashgate 1998) will be of interest to anybody wishing to read further. It uses Llewellyn's appointment to the Wiltshire Constabulary as a case study of the pre-1919 system, and although some biographical details are inaccurate these are not central to Dr Wall's theme.

Private Monograph: *Colonel Sir Hoël Llewellyn. A Life*, privately produced by B H Taylor of Banket, Zimbabwe, now the owner of Hoël Llewellyn's medals.
Magazines: I am particularly grateful to the editor and staff of the '*Police Review*' for access to back copies and other facilities. Other magazines consulted were, *Kewjay*, for article '*The Origins of the Wiltshire Constabulary*', (Issue No 9) Jan 1977 by Sgt P Smith. *The Field* Feb 1912, for Llewellyn's letter about police dogs.

ACKNOWLEDGEMENTS AND SOURCES

After the publication of the first edition of this book, the editor of the Police Historical Society Journal sent the author an article by Chris Forester, which tells the story of Llewellyn's sword.

Newspapers:

Local newspapers: '*Wiltshire Gazette*', '*Wilshire Times*', '*Wiltshire News*', '*Wiltshire Telegraph*', '*Wiltshire and Gloucestershire Standard*', 'Salisbury and Winchester Journal and General Advertiser', '*Salisbury Times and South Wiltshire Gazette*', '*North Wiltshire Herald*', '*Swindon Evening Advertiser*'.

National Newspapers: '*The Times*', '*Daily Mail*' and '*Daily Sketch*'.

Other Printed Works: *The Salisbury Diocesan Journal and Gazette, 1900-1935*, with thanks to Rev John Gosling of the Diocesan Library Committee, Crane Street Salisbury. *Great Western Railway timetable for 1913*, National Railway Museum, York. *Wiltshire Province Masonic Calendars. The History of All Saints Church, Burrington, Somerset.*

Reports: *Select Committee on Coroners Duties* HMSO 1910, *Home Office Committee on Death Certificates and Coroners* HMSO 1971. House of Commons Select Committee, Freemasonry in the Judiciary and Police HMSO 1997.

Official Archive Sources:

Wiltshire Archives

Constabulary Archives, Standing Joint Committee Minutes, Parish Registers, Wilsford and Enford, Minutes of the Enford Parish Council, 1913, Masonic Lodge Returns to The Clerk of the Peace, Wiltshire Quarter Sessions.

National Archives:

ADM1196143 (Naval Officer's Records), WO 374/42480 Army Personal File, W0/32/8155 Victoria Cross Recommendations to BSAP Personnel; War Office Archives, War Diary, 3rd County of London Yeomanry August 1915.

ACKNOWLEDGEMENTS AND SOURCES

National Army Museum, Chelsea:

Llewellyn Papers, NAM 9702-13

Special Thanks to:

Police Related Sources: Sergeant Anthony Rae, Lancashire Constabulary, Chairman of the UK Police Roll of Honour Trust, which is dedicated to recording the names of all policemen who have given their lives in the course of duty. Harry Wynne for details of the Durham police murders. John Ross, Curator of the Metropolitan Police Crime Museum (The 'Black Museum'). Brian H Taylor, ex-British South African Police. Major Tim Morley, ex-Wiltshire Constabulary.

Other Sources: Mr McGregor, Archivist at the Meteorological Office, Bracknell, for information about the weather in Wiltshire in March and April 1913. Gloria C Clifton, The Royal Observatory, for details of 1913 moon phases. British Telecom Archives for details of telephone subscribers in Wiltshire in 1913. Michael J C Burgess, Hon Secretary of the Coroners Society of England and Wales. David C Masters, HM Coroner for Wiltshire and Swindon. Mr David Fletcher at the Tank Museum, Bovington, Dorset. Ian Cross of Pietermaritzbug RSA, formerly a Rhodesian Resident Magistrate. Philip Davis, the great-nephew of Frank Crouch, for useful assistance. Christopher Pike and Jean Fenney, grandchildren of Ernest Pike. Oliver Pike. Lord Radnor and Paul Sylvester for their courtesy in answering my letters. Mr and Mrs Robertson, Churchwardens of St Nicholas' Wilsford. The late Mrs Ivy Punter. The House of Commons Information Service. Mr and Mrs R Thornton of Coombe. Major Chris Rose formerly of Peelers Cottage, Enford. The late Mrs Chadderton of Haxton for details of her father's recollection of the recovery of Ernest Pike's body. Alan Cook, former river keeper, of Netheravon. Alumni Office Trinity College Dublin for details of Keating's education. Pat Oborne, executor of the late Fred Phillimore. Reverend Canon Christopher Bryant, Master of St Nicholas Hospital Salisbury. Roland Ware of The Amesbury Society. Library and Museum staff Freemasons Hall,

ACKNOWLEDGEMENTS AND SOURCES

London. The Secretaries of the Grand Lodges of Scotland and Ireland. Mr A Money, Radley College Archivist. Home Office Record Management Services.

Mr Peter Beale, Historian, 9th Battalion Tank Corps. Mr W.E. Megaughy.

My apologies to anyone I may have overlooked.

Finally, but certainly not least, my thanks and apologies to my wife, Eileen for her help, tolerance and forbearance in the face of my obsession with this story.